THE THAMES PATH

St Paul's Cathedral from Bankside

THE THAMES PATH

by

Leigh Hatts

CICERONE PRESS
MILNTHORPE, CUMBRIA

ISBN 1 85284 270 9
A catalogue record for this book is available from the British Library.

ACKNOWLEDGEMENTS

The author is grateful for help from David Sharp, Jane Bowden, Rosemary Clarke, Stephen Green, James Hatts (for transport information), Jos Joslin, Marion Marples, Paul Newman and many others over many years.

Advice to Readers

Readers are advised that whilst every effort is taken by the author to ensure the accuracy of this guidebook, changes can occur which may affect the contents. It is advisable to check locally on transport, accommodation, shops etc but even rights-of-way can be altered.

The publisher would welcome notes of any such changes

Front cover: Windsor Castle from The Thames Path

CONTENTS

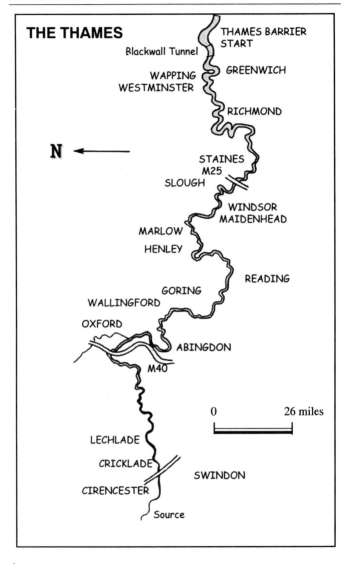

INTRODUCTION

Alternative Guide

This book is a guide for those walking 180 miles upstream along the Thames Path from London to Gloucestershire and is therefore an alternative to the official Countryside Commission guide designed to assist walkers heading from the river source downstream to the capital.

Many who know the river in London have dreamed of one day following the Thames to its source so Thames Path project officers have worked from east to west.

Towpath to National Trail

As early as the 1880s there was a suggestion that the Thames towpath, falling into disuse as traffic turned from the river to railways, should be preserved as a long distance recreational route. In the next century the call was taken up after the First World War by the Council for the Protection of Rural England and after the Second World War by the Thames Conservancy's River Thames Walk Committee. Thirty years later the Ramblers' Association and River Thames Society managed to persuade the Thames Water Authority and the Countryside Commission to produce a feasibility study on a continuous route from London to the Source making use of the remaining sections of towpath. This was eventually published in 1985 and government approval for the Thames Path was given in 1989. The route was officially opened, following the creation of 16 miles of new riverside path and three bridges, in 1996.

The 180 mile Thames Path from London to Gloucestershire is the only long distance route to follow a river throughout its length from tidal waters and also the only one to pass through London and major towns. Eighty-nine per cent of the Path is public footpath or bridleway.

London

The birth of a riverside path in London coincides with a realisation that the capital's waterway offers great opportunities both on and off the water. In the 1980s it looked as if the Thames might become merely a highway for barges taking London's rubbish downstream to Rainham or Mucking Marshes. However by 1986 the Pool of London had as many as 36 cruiseliners and naval vessels passing under Tower Bridge in a year. Now piers are being built for a riverbus service.

As many as 44 different birds have been recorded at the Thames Barrier where the national trail starts. The tidal-Thames, fishless at the start of the 20th century, is the cleanest metropolitan river in the world with an estuary supporting 115 species of fish and playing a part in supporting North Sea fish stocks. Salmon, extinct in Greater London since 1833 due to pollution, returned in the 1980s. Smelt, a cousin of the salmon which thrive in good water, congregate below Gravesend in winter and in spring come upstream in shoals to spawn at Wandsworth. Eels pass through central London in early summer. London now has an increasing number of swans although only a few years ago they were so scarce that the annual swan count was abandoned.

Upper Reaches
Long before the Thames turns non-tidal near the Greater London boundary the river becomes a green corridor running out of the capital. The upper reaches are varied. The water can be a busier highway than London at Maidenhead and Henley. Elsewhere, especially above Oxford, water and towpath can be both beautiful and lonely. Here accommodation and transport needs to be carefully planned.

In the Home Counties and even in far off Wiltshire there are reminders of London. Duchy of Lancaster territory is encountered around the Savoy and at Kempsford; Shelley knew the Thames from London to Lechlade and William Morris lived by the river both at Hammersmith and near the end of navigation at Kelmscot. Stone for St Paul's came downstream from Oxfordshire.

The Source
The climax to the 180 mile walk is an empty field with an often dry spring. Fortunately there is a nearby hidden pub with strong Thames connections and the first convenient railway station since Oxford.

Peace and Danger

The Thames has many moods. In London it offers peace among the chaos but it can also be the Dangerous Thames with fast currents and cold water. At low tide the beach at Hammersmith can suck a human into the mud. The non-tidal upper reaches also have deep waters and even crossing the tempting Duxford ford can be dangerous. More recently the drought has resulted in a slower water flow susceptible to freezing but still not safe to walk on.

Wildlife

Moorhens and voles are seen in quiet pools although they are at risk from the increase in mink which have no natural predator in Britain. Herons and cormorants are a familiar sight around Putney and even in Docklands. Ducks are found from at least Blackfriars. Deer will be encountered and still there are many reaches where cattle are watered at the river's natural bank.

River Authority

In 1197 Richard I, who was short of money after the Crusades, sold the river conservancy to the Corporation of London which in 1857 reluctantly handed it over to the Thames Conservancy Board. In fact the City had for much of the time laid little claim to the non-tidal Thames which by 1757 was controlled by Thames Navigation Commissioners who built the towpath. Since 1909 the 96 mile tidal Thames from Teddington to the sea has been under the control of the Port of London Authority. In 1974 Thames Conservancy, controlling the non-tidal river as far as Cricklade, was succeeded by the Thames Water Authority which gave way in 1989 to the even more short-lived National Rivers Authority. The present Environment Agency was formed in 1995.

Thames Path Officer

The Countryside Commission's Thames Path Officer is Jos Joslin who also looks after The Ridgeway which crosses the Thames at Goring. Her address is the National Trails Office, Countryside Service, Department of Leisure & Arts, Holton, Oxford OX33 1QQ (tel 01865 810224; fax 01865 810207; e-mail mail@rway-tpath.demon.co.uk). Flood information is available from the Environment Agency on 0645 881188.

Left and Right Banks

This Thames guide maintains tradition by referring to the left bank and right bank rather than the north and south bank. Banks can also be east and west. To check which is the left or right bank you should be looking downstream - or back towards London.

Diversions

This guide does include possible diversions such as at Culham to visit the attractive village of Sutton Courtenay on the Old Thames and at Pinkhill to use the towpath and summer ferry rather than the all season inland route. However, London's left bank alternative route, designated by the Countryside Commission as an afterthought, is not included as it is felt that long distance walkers will prefer the original right bank path which avoids traffic and affords a fine view of the City of London.

Accommodation

Each chapter includes a short accommodation list although returning to London each day by rail is easy as far as Oxford. *The Thames Path Practical Handbook*, issued by the National Trails Office, has over 200 addresses for bed & breakfast, camping and hostels. Accommodation lists are included on the Thames Path web-site: www.nattrails.gov.uk

Public Transport

Most of the Thames Path is easily accessible by public transport as indicated at the start of each section. Walkers using Thames Trains between stations on the Paddington-Oxford line should remember to ask for a Thames Path Cheap Day Return which allows for a return journey from a different station. A free leaflet *Public Transport to the Thames Path* is available from the National Trails Office (see above).

How Long?

Walking the Thames Path can easily take three weeks if time is spent exploring in every town and village. Some will take years by undertaking the route in short weekend sections. The Thames Path in summer is different from the Thames Path in winter, autumn or spring. Having walked one way there is a temptation to walk back and see new views.

Start of Thames Path at Thames Barrier

1. Thames Barrier to Tower Bridge

9 miles

The first section, which can easily be a day's walk if pauses are made at the landmarks, passes along the Greenwich waterfront and through Surrey Docks into central London. There are fine views of the Dome and the Isle of Dogs with its famous Canary Wharf Tower - the vertical Fleet Street - seen from many angles. The way from Woolwich Road in Charlton to the Thames Barrier start is signed as a Green Chain Path.

THAMES BARRIER The world's largest movable flood barrier, known as the 8th Wonder of the World, was built between 1974 and 1982 in response to the rising sea level which threatened to put London under water during a North Sea tidal surge. The nearby Visitors Centre is open daily. The first few yards of the Path are under cover and alongside a river profile map created by artist Simon Read.

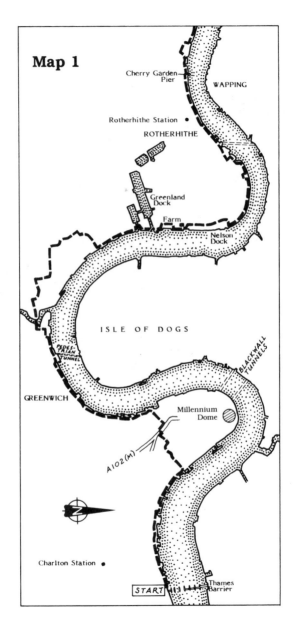

Map 1

Cherry Garden Pier

WAPPING

Rotherhithe Station

ROTHERHITHE

Greenland Dock

Farm

Nelson Dock

ISLE OF DOGS

PEDESTRIAN TUNNEL

BLACKWALL TUNNELS

GREENWICH

Millennium Dome

A102(M)

Charlton Station

START — Thames Barrier

The 180 mile route starts at the end of the promenade immediately downstream of the Thames Barrier where there is a notice over the Thames Path entrance. Follow the covered path and beyond the flood protection steps turn back to join a riverside path known as Hiroshima Walk. After The Anchor & Hope the path is marked by bricks in the road. Beyond Cory's bargeworks on Durham Wharf the road turns inland leaving the path to run ahead as Mudlarks Way. Soon the Way is round a gravel wharf to a point where another path joins from Horn Lane.

From this point to the Blackwall Tunnel main road there will be temporary diversions during 1999. The Thames Path is not due to run round the Dome on Blackwall Point until about 2002 when the Millennium Exhibition closes. (The original Thames Path route is: Ahead with the river; left down River Way passing The Pilot; right into cobbled Blackwall Lane and left to the main road.) During the Millennium celebration years the route will be ahead round the new Greenwich Yacht Club and by a natural riverside beach in front of an ecological park by the Millennium Village. The path will continue past the end of the new Mudlarks Boulevard. (River Way further along will be blocked off from the river.) Before the path reaches the Dome enclosure it will be necessary to go left on a path running south-west across the Blackwall peninsula, over two access roads, to the footbridge spanning the Blackwall Tunnel main road.

BLACKWALL POINT is the tip of the Greenwich Peninsula or Marsh which for almost a century was one of Europe's largest gasworks. Construction started in 1881 and included the most advanced gas holders. The tip is now the site of the Millennium Dome Exhibition. The new Jubilee Line Underground station will serve the 32 acre Millennium Village. Its pub is The Pilot which opened in 1805.The Blackwall Tunnel road link to the north bank was opened in 1897 for horse-drawn traffic.

Cross the footbridge and keep forward past two gantries to go left down the first alley leading to Blackwall Reach. There is a view across the water to Millwall Reach on the Isle of Dogs.

GREENWICH'S BLACKWALL REACH includes working wharves.

Morden Wharf is named after Sir John Morden who founded nearby Blackheath's Morden College in 1695. On Enderby's Wharf the Enderby brothers set up a rope walk in 1834 and during Antarctic whaling expeditions discovered Enderby Land and Greenwich Island. General Gordon, a relative, spent his last night in England at Enderby House built in 1846. The cobbled Ballast Quay, with its mid-Victorian Harbour Master's Office, is where ships took on Blackheath gravel as ballast for return voyages. The Cutty Sark Tavern dates from 1804.

ISLE OF DOGS, known as Stepney Marsh until Henry VIII had his kennels built there, was called an island before becoming a real island in 1805 when West India Dock was given an eastern entrance. Today's landmark is the 50 storey Canary Wharf Tower, Britain's tallest building, completed in 1991. Occupiers include the *Independent*, *Mirror* and *Telegraph* newspapers.

Follow the path to Ballast Quay. Shortly beyond The Cutty Sark Tavern there is the end of Hoskins Street. Turn the corner back to the river where the Thames Path crosses the Greenwich Meridian before passing the power station and reaching Trinity Hospital.

TRINITY HOSPITAL, home to 21 local men, was founded in 1613 by Lord Northampton whose tomb (by Nicholas Stone) is in the chapel having been moved from Dover about 1770. The battlements were added in 1812. High tides are recorded on the river wall. The adjoining power station was built in 1906 to supply London's trams.

Keep ahead along a passage behind High Bridge Wharf, passing High Bridge Drawdock and The Yacht, to find the Trafalgar Tavern.

TRAFALGAR TAVERN, opened in 1837, was famous for its annual whitebait dinner when the Prime Minister and cabinet arrived by barge. The fish was caught locally and cooked within the hour. Charles Dickens set the wedding breakfast in *Our Mutual Friend* here and artist Tissot featured the river frontage in 1878 sketches and an oil painting. The next door Curlew Rowing Club, founded in 1866, is the tideway's oldest.

Take the narrow path in front of Greenwich's Royal Naval College.

GREENWICH The former Royal Naval College buildings, now occupied by the University of Greenwich, are on the site of a Tudor palace where Henry VIII was born and married Catherine of Aragon. Wren's buildings, intended as a naval version of Chelsea Hospital, frame The Queen's House designed by Inigo Jones for James I's wife and built to span the line of the old main road. It is now part of the National Maritime Museum as is the Observatory on the hill. St Alphege's stands on the site of Archbishop Alphege's martyrdom by invading Danes in 1012. Composer Thomas Tallis and General Wolfe are buried inside. The *Cutty Sark* tea clipper, in dry dock since 1954, provides the skyline of masts for the townscape. Ye Olde Pie House, in Church Street, has been run by the Goddard family for four generations.

FOOT TUNNEL ALTERNATIVE The Greenwich foot tunnel is also part of the Thames Path which from here to Teddington at the end of the tidal Thames runs along both sides. This guide follows the original route on the south side.

Pass the *Cutty Sark* and foot tunnel entrance to reach where the path turns inland at Horseferry Place (landing point for the ferry until the tunnel opened in 1902). Go right, left at The Thames pub and right to cross Deptford Creek. The St Paul's Deptford steeple can be seen ahead.

DEPTFORD CREEK is the mouth of the River Ravensbourne which rises in Bromley. When the *Golden Hinde* moored here in 1581 Elizabeth I went on board to knight Sir Francis Drake. Both the road and rail bridges can open to let tall ships up river.

Once on the Deptford bank continue along the main road past The Hoy. At The Duke go right into Gonson Street and left into Stowage. The road rises slightly behind the site of the former power station to pass the back of the charnel house in Deptford's old churchyard.

ST NICHOLAS DEPTFORD has a medieval Kentish ragstone tower which was once a shipping landmark. Outside is the charnel house where bodies found in the river were stored. Among those buried in the churchyard is playwright Christopher Marlowe who was mysteriously murdered nearby in 1593. The gatepost sculls are crowned with wreaths symbolising victory over death. A new church was built off the High Street in 1730.

Keep ahead at the junction to pass Rachel McMillan Nursery School and McMillan's. (Continue to the end into the main road only if visiting Deptford High Street.) Before the main road go right on the path running across Hughes Fields. Keep right at a junction to reach Hughes Fields School ahead. (Look behind for a view of the spire of St Paul's Deptford.) Go left along the cobbled road and when this ends keep forward through Caravel Mews to Watergate Street - linking Deptford High Street (left) with the Thames.

DEPTFORD was a fishing village which Henry VIII turned into a naval dockyard. Trinity House, the coastal pilotage authority, started here as 'The Guild of the Most Glorious Trinity of Deptford'. Diarist John Evelyn lived at Sayes Court where in 1698 Peter The Great of Russia stayed incognito studying shipbuilding (hence Czar Street). Convoys Wharf, the last working dock, normally has plenty of paper imports cargo but as recently as 1995 Royal Artillery vehicles returning from abroad landed here. The ferry steps remain at the end of Watergate Street which is a continuation of the High Street, a rare survival of a 19th-century shopping street with two pie and mash shops and an entrance to Thomas Archer's outstanding St Paul's Church.

Go ahead into Princes Street to pass The Dog & Bell, Convoys Wharf and Czar Street. At The Globe by the main road turn right down a cobbled road at the side of Chester House to enter Sayes Court Park (the site of Evelyn's house). Bear left through the garden to reach Grove Street. Turn right to pass The Princess of Wales and go right into Leeway at the side of Pepys Park. Before the end take the park path on the left across the grass. Go up the wide stairs and through a gate on the left to follow a path to another gateway leading on to Deptford Strand.

DEPTFORD STRAND is the Royal Naval Dockyard site which from

1858 to 1961 was the Royal Victualling Yard. The riverfront buildings are former rum warehouses. A gateway to the offices of the Porter and Clerk of Cheque survive elsewhere on the housing estate named after Navy Secretary Samuel Pepys who had an office here in the 17th century. Across the river by the pier is Burrell's Wharf where Isambard Brunel's *Great Eastern* steamship was launched in 1858.

The promenade continues across St George's Wharf where a boundary stone marks the Deptford-Rotherhithe boundary. Go over South Dock's lock gates and right to pass the rebuilt Dog & Duck Stairs (named after a disappeared pub) by Greenland Pier. Continue along the riverside to the Greenland Dock entrance crossed by a swing bridge.

GREENLAND DOCK, named after its whaling connections and dating from 1700, was enlarged in 1904.

Stay on the riverfront along Swedish Quays and below King Frederick IX Tower to turn inland down Randall's Rents - not ahead on the wooden walkway.

RANDALL'S RENTS is named after John Randall who committed suicide in 1803 by jumping from a window of Nelson Dock House (see below). The alley, dating from 1698 and once called Wet Dock Lane, was lined with housing for workers of Randall's Shipyard which around 1800 was the second largest in London.

On reaching the back of The Ship & Whale go right to follow Odessa Street along the back of rebuilt New Caledonian Wharf. At the bend turn right on to Commercial Pier Wharf play area to find Barnard's Wharf.

BARNARD'S WHARF housing was completed in 1992. As Barnard's Dockyard there was a substantial dry dock here. Across the river is Seacon's Express Wharf where steel is unloaded - immediately upstream was a deep water timber wharf until 1994.

Beyond the animal sculptures go through Surrey Docks Farm. (If gates are locked go through estate and right to follow road round to farm entrance.)

SURREY DOCKS FARM, which started on the south side of Greenland Dock entrance in 1975 and moved here in 1986, is run on organic lines with eggs, cheese, honey and goats milk on sale. At night two farm dogs keep foxes away. The café is open daily except Mondays.

Walk ahead along Rotherhithe Street past Trinity Wharf to go right up an avenue of trees on to Durand's Wharf. This leads on to Lawrence Wharf but until there is a continuous riverside path in front of the Holiday Inn ahead it is necessary to go left and stay in Rotherhithe Street as far as Canada Wharf which is just beyond Nelson Dock.

NELSON DOCK takes its name from Nelson Wake who rented the dock in the 1820s. When Nelson Dock House was built in 1740 it faced fields and was flanked by timber yards. (Logs were landed at downstream Lawrence Wharf until 1986.) Between 1687 and 1888 at least 114 ships were built here including naval gun ships. From the 1750s until 1821 Randall & Brent pioneered steam shipbuilding and in the 1850s Bilbe & Perry pioneered timber cladding on iron frames for China tea clippers. The yard closed in 1968 and in 1989 the dock was renamed Port Nelson and flats built. When they failed to sell the complex became a hotel (now Holiday Inn) and reverted to its original name. The large dry dock has a caisson which may be a ship's stern - best seen from the pier. In the small dock there is a French Navy training vessel which once carried tourists around the Channel Islands. Upstream Columbia Wharf (part of the hotel) is a late Victorian granary.

Continue along the road at the back of Columbia and Canada Wharves (passing The Blacksmiths Arms) to turn up an alley known as Horn Stairs.

HORN STAIRS, once known as Cuckold's Point, probably takes its name from the ducking stool here (on the Canada Wharf site) which had a set of horns on top of its wooden structure as late as the 1750s. Downstream Canada Wharf is a former timber warehouse. The upstream houses were built in 1994-5 on Ordnance Wharf leadworks which closed in 1982 and Sunderland Wharf.

Continue along the riverside to pass a decorative obelisk and Pageants Stairs. After a short distance cross the former Lavender Dock entrance to reach Sovereign View. Across the street to the left is the now much reduced Lavender Pond.

SOVEREIGN VIEW, a housing development completed in 1993, covers the former Lavender Wharf occupied until 1985 by Burmah Castrol's oil depot. In the 18th century the site had been occupied by shipwrights. Lavender Pond behind the dock entrance is a two acre nature park formed from the remains of a vast dock of the same name. The pumphouse re-opened in 1991 as the Rotherhithe Heritage Museum displaying the result of local beach combing and dockers' tools (open Wednesday-Sunday). Across the river is the entrance to Limehouse Basin and the London canal system.

At Globe Stairs the path returns to the road opposite The Three Compasses. Turn right to walk round Globe Wharf.

GLOBE WHARF RICE MILL was built in 1883 and for almost a century the six storey building handled all rice coming into London.

Turn right up the far side of Globe Wharf to walk along King & Queen Wharf which leads on to Prince's Riverside.

PRINCE'S RIVERSIDE is the former Bellamy's Wharf aggregates depot which closed in 1992 to be redeveloped as flats with the riverside path running on a bridge across the dock inlet. At the far end there is Bull Head Dock Wharf, once specialising in ship breaking and resale of timbers, where the *Téméraire* was broken up. The 320 bed Youth Hostel behind opened in 1991.

On returning to the road go right past the Youth Hostel to cross the Surrey Basin Entrance drawbridge.

SURREY BASIN ENTRANCE gave access to nine other major docks. The first ship entered in 1807. Spice Island pub, resembling a boathouse and built in 1995 on Dinorwic Wharf, recalls the spice trade.

Cross the drawbridge ahead and just beyond Octagon Court (right) go right up steps on to Clarence Wharf.

CLARENCE WHARF belonged to Surrey Consumers' Gas Company. The pier was built in 1860 for the landing of coal for the gasworks which closed in 1959. Sea-dredged aggregates, which were unloaded at high tide into hoppers running above the street, replaced coal until the wharf closed in 1992. The riverside path opened in 1997 shortly after Brunel Point housing development was completed. Restoration of the pier for public access was part of the planning consent.

Just past Isambard Close turn right on to Cumberland Wharf which at the far end has a statue recalling the Pilgrim Fathers. Return to Rotherhithe Street, to pass a former barge builders and the Brunel tunnel house (left).

ROTHERHITHE was a market garden village which became a shipbuilding centre. The church was rebuilt in 1715 but in the crypt is a medieval base incorporating Roman bricks. The interior pillars are ships' masts and the Epiphany Chapel altar is made from *Téméraire* wood (see below). To the left of the sanctuary is a plaque to Captain Christopher Jones of the Pilgrim Fathers' *Mayflower* which in 1620 sailed to America from the jetty behind The Mayflower (once licensed to sell British and US stamps to visiting sailors). It opened as The Shippe in 1515 and as The Spread Eagle it was used during 1825-43 by men digging Brunel's Thames Tunnel ('the Great Bore') intended as a foot and horse crossing but converted for trains in 1865-9 (now the East London Line). The Rotherhithe road tunnel opened in 1908 after 3,000 people had been moved. Although the docks closed in 1970 two Scandinavian churches remain in Albion Street. The toilets at the end of the street have Men and Women signs in Norwegian and English. In Rotherhithe churchyard is the Wilson family tomb containing the body of Prince Lee Boo of the Pelau Islands who sailed here in the 1780s with Captain Wilson. Rotherhithe is the childhood home of actor Michael Caine and entertainer Max Bygraves.

Rotherhithe Street narrows to run between warehouses including Hope Sufferance Wharf. At a junction go right to climb steps. Beyond King's Stairs the path is in an arcade with the first view of Tower Bridge. A little further on the way is briefly blocked by the former Braithwaite & Dean's lighterage office -

once part of a terrace. The Angel marks the end of Rotherhithe Street.

THE ANGEL, dating from at least 1682, is the successor to The Salutation on the site run by nearby Bermondsey Abbey. Samuel Pepys and Captain Cook both visited. The painter James Whistler sketched Rotherhithe from the balcony reputed to be haunted by Judge George Jeffreys who watched the executions on Wapping beach opposite. Across the road are the remains of Edward III's palace - hence nearby King's Stairs.

Continue past the palace and along Bermondsey Wall East to reach Cherry Garden Pier.

CHERRY GARDEN PIER was used in 1664 by Samuel Pepys visiting the pleasure garden. Later it was popular with those taking the waters at Bermondsey Spa in the 1760s. The pier was J.M.W. Turner's vantage point for his painting *The Fighting Téméraire* showing the Trafalgar ship arriving at sunset to be broken up. The cottages in Wilson Grove (running south) were built in 1928 at the instigation of local doctor and MP Alfred Salter whose life-size figure can be seen sitting on a riverside seat waving at his daughter and a cat.

At Fountain Green Square turn inland to rejoin Bermondsey Wall East. The way round Chambers Wharf cold store is down Loftie Street, right into Chambers Street and right again up East Lane to East Lane Stairs.

EAST LANE STAIRS, also known as Sterling Wharf Stairs, is a lightermen's landing point. Number 33 on the west side was built in 1866 and used as a grain store.

Follow Bermondsey Wall West where, beyond St Saviour's House, the area inland is known as Jacob's Island. Ahead is the sharp turn into Mill Street.

MILL STREET is one side of St Saviour's Dock. The 1885 New Concordia Wharf flour mill was one of Docklands' first conversions, being begun in 1980 when Vogan's Mill pea-splitting, pearl barley and lentil mills still operated with Spillers dog biscuit factory opposite. Ship's biscuit manufacturer George Frean founded Peak-

Freans in 1858 in Mill House (south of Wolesey Street) where Garibaldi biscuits were first made. Jacob Street marks the centre of Jacob's Island - once a slum surrounded by stagnant water ditches fed by the diverted Neckinger stream (see Dock below) and depicted in Charles Dickens' *Oliver Twist*. In 1849 *The Morning Chronicle* described this area as "the Venice of drains" and "the very capital of Cholera".

The Path does not go sharp left with the road into Mill Street but ahead into the New Concordia Wharf to bear right through a passage. Cross St Saviour's Dock to reach Tea Trade Wharf on the corner of the Dock and the beginning of Butler's Wharf.

ST SAVIOUR'S DOCK was formed by the mouth of the now diverted River Neckinger on which Bermondsey Abbey had a tide-mill. 'Neckinger' is said to come from 'neckcloth' with which pirates were hanged here. Shad Thames, behind the western warehouses, is the best preserved dockland canyon street where the last working spice mill provided the original aroma until 1994. Cinnamon Wharf has been rebuilt to a Michael Hopkins design for David Mellor whose kitchenware shop was briefly here. Tea Trade Wharf on the north-west end was built in 1922. The unobstrusive pedestrian swingbridge was thrown across in 1996 and is open daily 7am to 10pm (11pm in summer).

BUTLER'S WHARF is a collection of former bonded warehouses. A man who worked here in 1937 said: "We had just about everything coming through...rubber, cocoa, coffee, cassia, cardamons, canned salmon, ginger, dates, nutmeg, wines, spirits..." About 6,000 tea chests a day was normal and now there is a Tea & Coffee Museum in the Clove Building behind the Design Museum. The next door warehouse is one of the last timber-framed examples in Docklands. After the wharf closed in 1972 some buildings were used as studios by artists David Hockney and David Gentleman and the streets as a film set for *The French Lieutenant's Woman* and *Dr Who*. The main building, dating from 1875, includes Terence Conran's Le Pont de la Tour restaurant (where Tony Blair and President Clinton once dined) and a bakery. At the west end is the former Courage brewery which operated here from 1789 until 1981. The view is of St Katharine's Wharf and the Tower Thistle Hotel.

Walk along Spice Wharf promenade to pass the restaurant and pier. Narrow Maggie Blake's Cause takes the path back to Shad Thames. Go right to Tower Bridge.

Refreshments

Ballast Quay: Cutty Sark Tavern. 11am-11pm. (Sun 12-10.30pm.) Food 12-9pm (Sat 7pm).

Greenwich: Goddard's Ye Olde Pie House, Church Street, near *Cutty Sark*. 11an-3.30pm except Mon.

Surrey Docks Farm: Café open daily 10am-5pm except Mon.

Nelson Dock: Holiday Inn. Breakfast from 7am & other meals.

Surrey Docks Entrance: Spice Island pub open 11am-11pm with food served until 9pm.

Rotherhithe: The Mayflower, Rotherhithe Street. 12-11pm. Bar snacks until 6pm. (Sun 12-10.30pm).

Rotherhithe: Finnish Church Cafeteria, Albion Street. 3-9.30pm Wed-Fri. 1-9.30pm weekends.

Butler's Wharf: Tea & Coffee Museum café, next to Design Museum. 10am-6pm.

Accommodation

Nelson Dock: Holiday Inn (0171 231 1001).

Rotherhithe: YHA (0171 232 2114).

Transport

Thames Barrier: Rail (Connex) to Charlton.

Tower Bridge: Underground from Tower Hill.

Map

OS Landranger 177 (East-London).

HMY Britannia seen from Tower Bridge

2. Tower Bridge to Putney
10 miles

This section takes the Path from the Pool of London through central London by way of Bankside, the South Bank, Lambeth Palace, Battersea and Wandsworth to the start of the towpath at Putney. The views are of the City of London and St Paul's Cathedral, the Palace of Westminster, Chelsea and Fulham.

TOWER BRIDGE, completed in 1894 with the drawbridges' weights in steel towers clothed in gothic style stone, was raised more than 6,000 times in its first year. Now it opens about 500 times. Two resident cats continue to keep the mice down. The public is admitted to the interior daily 10am-5.15pm (4pm winter); admission charge.

From below the south end of Tower Bridge turn upstream into Potters Fields facing the Tower of London.

POTTERS FIELDS recalls Roman pottery found here. The park

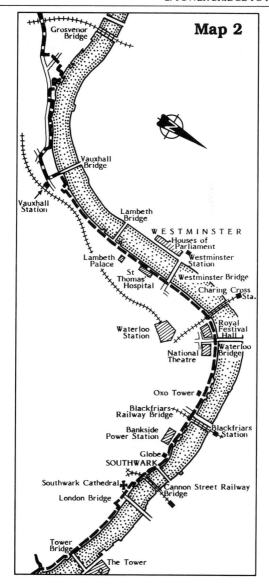

Map 2

Grosvenor Bridge

Vauxhall Bridge

Vauxhall Station

Lambeth Bridge

WESTMINSTER

Houses of Parliament

Westminster Station

Lambeth Palace

St Thomas' Hospital

Westminster Bridge

Charing Cross Sta.

Royal Festival Hall

Waterloo Station

Waterloo Bridge

National Theatre

Oxo Tower

Blackfriars Railway Bridge

Bankside Power Station

Blackfriars Station

Globe

SOUTHWARK

Southwark Cathedral

Cannon Street Railway Bridge

London Bridge

Tower Bridge

The Tower

opened in 1988 embracing a burial ground (tombstones in south corner) and Pickle Herring Street which continued westwards from under Tower Bridge behind wharves overlooking the Tower of London.

TOWER OF LONDON dates from William the Conqueror's reign. The moat, fed by the Thames, was added 200 years later and only filled in during the 19th century on the orders of the Duke of Wellington.

Continue past the permanently moored HMS *Belfast* and Southwark Crown Court to reach Hay's Wharf.

HAY'S WHARF was started in 1651 by Alexander Hay who bought the Abbot of Battle's Inn (once the Abbot's London house) on the site of Hay's Galleria - the 1850s inlet dock turned shopping arcade. The Horniman recalls the tea clippers which called here from 1862 - in 1950 a million tea chests were landed. New Zealand butter and cheese started arriving in 1867 and Hay's became 'London's Larder' until closure in 1970. In 1987 it re-opened as London Bridge City but the east end is yet to be completed on the site of Edward II's Rosary Palace and a house built by Sir John Fastolfe (Shakespeare's 'Falstaff'). At the west end is the Wharf offices, St Olaf House, built in 1931 to Goodhart-Rendel's continental-modern design on the site of St Olave's Church. Across the water is the Custom House and former Billingsgate fish market.

Beyond the pier but before London Bridge leave the Pool of London by turning down a narrow path by St Olaf House and go right to pass under London Bridge to Southwark Cathedral.

LONDON BRIDGE, completed in 1973, replaces Rennie's 1831 bridge which is now in Arizona. Its predecessors, starting with the Romans' wooden structure and including those with houses on, were a few yards downstream. The inland archway on the Southwark bank is all that remains here of the 1831 bridge. The Lord Mayor of London is entitled to any sturgeon caught below London Bridge.

SOUTHWARK CATHEDRAL, London's oldest gothic church, has only been a cathedral since 1905. Originally a convent founded by St Swithun and then an Augustinian priory, its church became a parish church known to William Shakespeare - his brother is buried in the chancel. The Harvard Chapel recalls the local butcher's son who founded the university.

At the cathedral's west end turn right to pass St Mary Overie Dock (home of the *Golden Hinde* replica) and enter Clink Street by the palace ruin.

WINCHESTER PALACE The roofless dining hall with its 1370 rose window is the remains of the Bishop of Winchester's residence. The south bank was within the diocese and the bishop had a house here from 1109 until 1626. Henry VIII visited and Mary I and her new husband Philip of Spain landed here to dine before entering the City opposite. Clink Street recalls the 'Clink' prison beneath the kitchens. The palace parkland ran west almost to the present Blackfriars Bridge.

Continue ahead to pass the Clink Museum and go under Cannon Street Railway Bridge. At the junction turn right to rejoin the river at The Anchor.

THE ANCHOR There was a pub here on the Bishop's estate in Shakespeare's time. Samuel Pepys came to watch the Great Fire of London across the water. Dr Johnson stayed at the present pub and young Charles Dickens knew its exterior as a child. On the river here in 1989, between Cannon Street and Southwark Bridges, *The Marchioness* pleasure craft sank after hitting the sand dredger *Bowbelle*.

Continue along the waterside to the Financial Times building and go under Southwark Bridge.

SOUTHWARK BRIDGE The 1920s bridge replaces the 1819 toll crossing featured in Charles Dickens' *Little Dorrit*. At the upstream north end is Vintners' Hall rebuilt in 1992 to a design inspired by St Peter's Rome.

A short distance beyond the bridge is the area associated with the theatre.

BEAR GARDENS is an alley crossing the site of the Hope Theatre which staged bear baiting and plays in Elizabeth I's reign. Ben

Jonson's *Bartholomew Fair* was premiered here in 1614. The Shakespeare Education Centre contains its successor theatre. In the wall at the river end is a ferryman's seat.

THE GLOBE is a reconstruction completed in 1996 of Shakespeare's theatre which stood nearby (behind the FT) in Park Street from 1599 to 1644. The Bishop of Winchester was willing to let out his parkland for actors, unlike the hostile City of London opposite. Resident cats Brutus and Portia keep mice away.

CARDINAL CAP ALLEY is the last of the medieval passages leading from the river. Cardinal's Wharf was a pub where ferrymen met. Next door is now the Provost of Southwark's residence - the only deanery to have a view of the wrong cathedral. The looming power station is due to open as part of the Tate Gallery. The isolated pier was once used by oil tankers delivering to the power station.

Follow the promenade to reach The Founders Arms, marking the end of the Bishop of Winchester's land, to go under the bridges.

BLACKFRIARS BRIDGES abut the former Paris Garden mentioned in Shakespeare's play *Henry VIII*. The first road bridge, opened in 1769, was named William Pitt Bridge but people preferred 'Blackfriars' after the monastery at the confluence of the Rivers Fleet and Thames on the north side. The Fleet emerges under the present 1869 bridge below the spot where Italian banker Robert Calvi was found hanged in 1982. The railway bridge dates from 1884. Between the two are the piers of the first railway bridge erected in 1862 to carry the main continental trains and demolished in 1985. Its fine insignia survives in front of Express Newspapers' Ludgate House standing on the site of the burned out (1803) Albion flour mill which may have been the "dark satanic mills" in Blake's hymn *Jerusalem*. Doggett's Coat & Badge, named after the annual rowing race which has passed here since 1715, opened in 1977. The foot tunnel under Blackfriars road bridge opened in 1995.

Pass under the bridges to Doggett's and along King's Reach to Oxo Tower Wharf and the gardens.

OXO TOWER WHARF The tower was built in 1930 as London's

second highest commercial building with the OXO windows avoiding planning restrictions on advertising. The main building is older and was once known as River Plate Wharf. The top floor is now a Harvey Nichols restaurant. Members of the public may visit the public viewing section of the roof terrace. Immediately upstream is Old Barge House Stairs recalling Henry VIII's boatsheds and marking the end of the Paris Garden whose boundary can be traced along Broadwall inland from the *Hello!* magazine offices. To the west was Prince's Meadow marsh owned by the Duchy of Cornwall until 1953. Bernie Spain Gardens, immediately west and replacing Nelson's Wharf and Eldorado's ice cream factory, is named after local campaigner Bernadette Spain who died in 1984 - the year Coin Street Community Builders was formed to save the OXO Tower and replace 13 acres of derelict land with co-op housing. The riverside walk was opened by The Queen in 1988 when she walked from here to the Royal Festival Hall.

Follow the Queen's Walk to pass the London Television Centre and the National Theatre.

LONDON TELEVISION CENTRE is home of Carlton, LWT and GMTV. ITV's morning 'Richard and Judy' programme has a live river backdrop. The London *Today / Tonight* news studio can be seen on the main building's third floor where the glass wall allows for a spectacular panoramic backdrop. The site was a timber yard in the 1840s. Across the water is the Temple with Somerset House to the west. Moored at Temple steps is the 1927 PLA survey ship *St Katharine*.

Continue to Waterloo Bridge which cuts through the South Bank Centre.

WATERLOO BRIDGE The first opened in 1817 having been planned as Strand Bridge before the Battle in 1815. The present bridge by Giles Gilbert Scott was built in the late 1930s complete with explosion chambers in case of invasion.

SOUTH BANK CENTRE embraces the National Theatre, National Film Theatre, Museum of Moving Image, the Hayward Gallery and the Royal Festival Hall. The RFH was built for the 1951 Festival of Britain when the name South Bank was first used. Until 1962 a 140ft shot tower which produced shot for cartridges (1829-1948) stood at the north end of the RFH. Making way for the RFH was the Red Lion Brewery which for a time used river water for the brewing. The view is of The Savoy.

Go under Hungerford Bridge to pass Jubilee Gardens and County Hall.

HUNGERFORD BRIDGE was a Brunel suspension bridge opened in 1845 and sold in 1859 to the London SE Railway when the foot crossing was included as a planning condition. The railway claimed that few used it in summer due to the river's stench. Brunel's brick piers remain but the chains were removed to complete his Clifton suspension bridge in Bristol.

JUBILEE GARDENS, created in the Jubilee Year 1977, was part of the Festival of Britain site. In the 17th century it was a beach reclaimed for willow beds and an asparagus garden.

THE COUNTY HALL, recently converted into hotels, flats and an aquarium, was completed in 1933 after over 20 years' building to be home of the London County Council (GLC from 1965) until 1985. The site included Crosse & Blackwell Wharf. The lion at the far end comes from the top of the Lion Brewery on the RFH site.

Just before the lion a tunnel takes the Path under Westminster Bridge.

WESTMINSTER BRIDGE was the first between Putney and London when opened in 1750 despite attempted sabotage by ferrymen working a crossing dating from the days when the Palace of Westminster and Abbey were on an island formed by the Thames and ditches filled by the Tyburn River which turned the mill on Millbank. The present bridge, complementing the Victorian gothic Houses of Parliament, opened in 1861 with the Thames Path tunnel added in 1997.

Follow the Albert Embankment in front of the hospital with a fine view of the Houses of Parliament.

ST THOMAS' HOSPITAL, founded in Southwark by the monks of Southwark Cathedral, is dedicated to both St Thomas à Becket and

St Thomas the Apostle - so Thomas' is pronounced 'Thomases'. The hospital moved here to reclaimed land in 1871 with the original buildings being based on a French hospital visited by Florence Nightingale. A museum named after her is in the new building.

Just before Lambeth Bridge there is a famous view back to the Palace of Westminster. Across the road is Lambeth Palace.

LAMBETH PALACE has been the Archbishop of Canterbury's official residence since 1197. The gatehouse was built in 1495. The adjoining St Mary-at-Lambeth Church is now the Museum of Gardening History. Charles I's gardener John Tradescant and his son, who brought many now popular plants to England, are buried in the churchyard along with Captain Bligh of mutiny fame.

LAMBETH BRIDGE succeeded the Archbishop's horseferry (hence Horseferry Road opposite) used by Queen Mary and her baby (the Old Pretender) when fleeing abroad in 1688. The ferry ceased when Westminster Bridge opened and a bridge here (foot toll ¹/₂d) was not built until 1861. The present crossing, completed in 1932, is decorated with the pineapples introduced by John Tradescant the Younger. **On the upstream north end is MI5's HQ identified by aerials.**

The Path runs under the bridge to join the road in front of the Fire Service HQ which has a pier for fireboats. The chimneys of Battersea Power Station (reached later) can be seen behind the Tate Gallery on the far bank.

TATE GALLERY, the gift of sugar magnate Henry Tate, opened in 1897 with 67 paintings on the site of the Millbank Penitentiary which had been erected on the marshy land in 1821.

Stay by the river as the road veers away at Peninsula Heights.

PENINSULA HEIGHTS, built in 1962 as Alembic House and intended for the United Nations, was re-named in 1995 because the view east from author Jeffrey Archer's much photographed flat gives the feeling of being above the Thames. Former residents include actors Stanley Baker and Richard Harris. The next door Tintagel and Camelford Houses are a reminder that this is part of the Duchy of Cornwall's Kennington Manor.

Beyond Lack's Drawdock the path is in front of the Vauxhall Cross building. Go up the steps on to Vauxhall Bridge. (Turn right for a few yards only to see the confluence with the Effra.)

VAUXHALL BRIDGE was opened in 1816 as Regent's Bridge but at the turn of the century was replaced by the present structure decorated with bronze figures. The River Effra, which rises in Norwood and gives its name to Brixton's Effra Road, flows unseen under the Path between the bridge and the huge M16 building by Terry Farrell called Vauxhall Cross (but also known as 'Spooksville') and completed in 1993. 'Vauxhall' is derived from 'Faulkes Hall' built in about 1200 for Faulkes de Breaute. Between 1660 and 1859 Vauxhall was well known for its pleasure garden lying between Golding Street, Laud Street, Kennington Lane and St Oswald Place. In 1864 the Pearson-designed St Peter's Church was built next to the manager's house which became the vicarage. The altar marks the site of Neptune's Fountain. A rural air is now maintained by the city farm within the garden boundary. Doulton pottery was founded in Vauxhall Walk in 1815 and remained until 1956. Brunswick House, near the river, was built in 1758 by the Dawson family who ran a timber wharf behind.

Cross Vauxhall Bridge via the footbridge over the bridge approach and follow the main road upstream to go right at the side of Brunswick House. Just beyond Nine Elms Cold Store go right to the river. Ahead is a view of Westminster Cathedral tower. The riverside path (William Henry Walk) leads to Elm Quay.

ELM QUAY has a representation of Old Father Thames by Stephen Duncan (1988). Opposite is Dolphin Square, Europe's biggest block of flats completed in 1937, where tenants have included Princess Anne and numerous MPs. The modern house to the right, next to Pimlico Gardens, was completed in 1995 for the Sheikh of Dubai's cousin.

At the end continue along the main road and go right at Federal Express to reach Nine Elms Marina.

Chelsea Harbour and Battersea houseboats

Richmond
Hampton Ferry

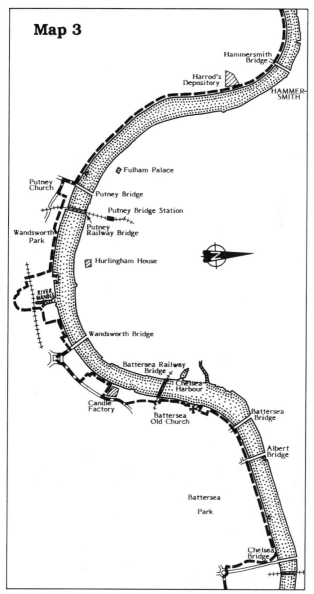

Map 3

Hammersmith Bridge

Harrod's Depository

HAMMER-SMITH

Fulham Palace

Putney Church

Putney Bridge

Putney Bridge Station

Putney Railway Bridge

Wandsworth Park

Hurlingham House

RIVER WANDLE

Wandsworth Bridge

Battersea Railway Bridge

Chelsea Harbour

Candle Factory

Battersea Old Church

Battersea Bridge

Albert Bridge

Battersea Park

Chelsea Bridge

NINE ELMS MARINA The Battersea barge *Maria*, built in Holland in 1931, carried grain on the Seine until seized by the Nazis. In 1979 she crossed the Channel to first become a floating restaurant at Lymington before coming up the Thames in 1987. Coal barges used to unload at Nine Elms Pier for Vauxhall Gasworks until 1971. A regular visitor here was the sand dredger *Bowbelle*.

The path goes round an inlet and past Nine Elms Pier to come up against an aggregates wharf and Battersea Power Station, forcing an inland diversion. Turn right along Kirtling Street which bends to go over a crossroads. At the end bear left to the main road and turn right. Keep on the main Battersea Park Road over the railway and past Battersea Dogs' Home to bear right along Prince of Wales Drive. At the roundabout cross the end of Prince of Wales Road (leading to Chelsea Bridge) to enter Battersea Park. Bear right to find the Wilderness blocking out sight and sound of the traffic.

BATTERSEA PARK opened in 1853 after the marshland had been raised with soil from the new Royal Victoria Dock. The Buddhist peace pagoda was erected in 1985. The riverside path has a view of Chelsea and its Royal Hospital - the gap in the houses is the once waterside Physic Garden. Chelsea was possibly the capital of Mercia from the 6th to 9th century.

On reaching the river bear left to join the path leading to Albert Bridge at the far end.

ALBERT BRIDGE had its strength questioned just 11 years after its 1873 opening but it has survived with its central prop eventually added in 1873. The only other example of this rigid chain design is in Prague. The toll booths, closed since 1879, and the 3,000 bulbs which illuminate the bridge at night give a seaside pier appearance.

Cross the road to find the path continuing by the toll booth. Beyond Ransom Dock Entrance pass architect Norman Foster's in-house designed glass office opened in 1990. Chelsea Old Church is across the water. Ahead is Battersea Bridge.

BATTERSEA BRIDGE The first was a 1771 wooden structure called 'Chelsea Bridge' and then 'Old Chain Bridge' which replaced a 200 year old ferry. Turner and Whistler both depict the bridge which was succeeded by the present one in 1890.

Cross the road to follow Morgan's Walk.

MORGAN'S WALK is named after the Morgan Crucible works which was here. Opposite are Chelsea's famous houseboats (rising twice a day with the tide) and London Transport's Lots Road Power Station built in 1905 for the District Line.

At the end of Morgan's Walk turn inland to avoid the Montevectro Building.

MONTEVECTRO BUILDING, designed by Richard Rogers, will contain 100 apartments when completed in 1999. The site was occupied by the landmark Hovis Flour Mill built in 1887 with a river frontage added in 1916. Grain arrived by barge until the late 1980s. The mill was sold in 1994 with the expectation that the existing building would be converted but demolition followed in 1997. There had been a mill here since 1794.

Until the Montevectro riverside path opens it is necessary to go inland and right to reach Battersea Church where there is river access.

BATTERSEA OLD CHURCH The window commemorating William Blake's wedding here (six years after the church was rebuilt in 1776) was dedicated in the presence of former Prime Minister Harold Wilson in 1979. The Curtis window includes a map showing lost riverside gardens. Turner often painted sunsets from the west room where the view is now of Chelsea Harbour begun in 1986 on the site of a railway goods yard. Cargo was unloaded in Chelsea Creek which is the borough boundary so the development (where Michael Caine, Tom Stoppard and Elton John were early residents) is in Fulham and not Chelsea.

Continue past the drawdock and turn right on to cobbled Vicarage Walk. When the flats end there is a view of Old Battersea House.

OLD BATTERSEA HOUSE, built in 1899, was recently the home of American publisher Malcolm Forbes who lent it to ex-President

Ronald Reagan. Forbes' son inherited the house which contains a fine art collection and, Forbes believed, the ghost of an old lady.

The path passes between The River Rat pub and Albion Quay's houseboats before reaching a railway bridge.

BATTERSEA RAILWAY BRIDGE opened in 1863 to carry both standard and Great Western Railway broad gauge trains between Clapham and Willesden Junctions. Now Eurostar trains can be seen running between Waterloo and North Pole depot.

The Path continues inland along a road running under the bridge. Beyond the heliport entrance turn right into York Road to reach Price's Candle factory.

PRICE'S CANDLES began here in 1830 as a coconut pressing factory but soon Queen Victoria's wedding brought a demand for cheap candles which were partly made of coconut fat. Palm oil, from the company's 1,000 acre coconut plantation in Ceylon (Sri Lanka), was landed from barges at low tide. Candles may be purchased at the shop. York Place is a reminder that in Tudor times the candle factory site was the London residence of the Archbishop of York with water on two sides - the Falcon Brook flowed into the now disappeared Battersea Creek on the downstream side.

Turn right into York Place, at the side of Price's, to reach Plantation Wharf.

PLANTATION WHARF was built as an office development but went into receivership before being turned into flats in 1993. Once sugar cane was landed here from barges sent up from the docks - hence Molasses House. Adjoining were Mendip and Sherwood timber wharves.

Continue on to Riverside Plaza on the old timber wharves and turn inland to walk across the piazza between Sherwood and Mendip Courts. At Chatfield Road go right and left into Mendip Road. At the main road go right to reach a roundabout by Wandsworth Bridge approach. Use the underpass (down the slope, left, right and right up slope) to emerge near a 24 hour McDonalds restaurant (left). Continue ahead towards Wandsworth Bridge beyond the bus stop.

WANDSWORTH BRIDGE opened in 1940 to replace the original 1873 crossing.

Just past Jews Row go left down steps at the side of the bridge to Pier Terrace. Follow the short cobbled road to pass The Ship Inn.

SHIP INN, opened about 1786, nearly closed in 1981 but 10 years later it was Pub of the Year. The sign shows the ship on which Sir Allen Young (of Young's Brewery fame) explored the North-West Passage in the 1870s. The barge *Convoy* was built at Rye in 1909 and occasionally sails downstream. The land immediately upstream was a gasworks. The new promenade is on the line of a travelling crane which ran between the river and a large coal bunker belonging to the gasworks.

Go right down the far side of the pub to reach the promenade. At the far end the path runs above the Refuse Transfer Station to the River Wandle.

REFUSE TRANSFER STATION opened in 1984 as Europe's most advanced. 4,000 tons of refuse are taken by water to Rainham and Mucking Marshes in Essex each week. A century ago the site was Feathers Wharf with an inn and tea garden.

Until the high path running above the refuse station is opened walkers must go left down a straight path - St Anne's pepper pot tower can be seen in the distance. Go right along the back of the refuse station on a road which becomes The Causeway and crosses the River Wandle - its confluence with the Thames can be seen to the right - to Causeway Island which is partly a nature reserve. The path bears left to go under the railway line and over the water flowing from the Wandle into Bell Lane Creek on the west side of the island. Keep ahead to reach The Crane at Wandsworth.

WANDSWORTH takes its name from the River Wandle which rises in Croydon and features in Izaak Walton's *The Compleat Angler*. There was a corn tide-mill at the Wandle's mouth in the mid 1760s. Above the first road bridge, the riverbank is occupied by Young's Brewery dating from 1581 and in the family since 1831. Coal and malt no longer arrive by barge, but dray horses, who deliver locally, are stabled at the brewery. Author H.G. Wells was married at All Saints where the tower dates from 1630.

Go ahead past Young's Crane pub and a row of cottages to go right into Frogmore. Turn right into Sudlow Road and left along North Passage to a junction opposite The Queen Adelaide. Turn right to go under the righthand railway bridge and up Point Pleasant to pass Prospect Cottages and Osiers Road. Just before the river there is The Cat's Back pub (right) and Prospect House (left).

PROSPECT HOUSE was built about 1805 for Joseph Gattey, owner of a nearby vinegar works. The road known as Point Pleasant existed in the 1730s. Prospect Quay, formerly a Calor Gas depot with a jetty, was developed in 1996 as flats with an extended pier for houseboats. Immediately upstream is the former Shell Oil Terminal.

Go ahead to the riverside and left along the front of Prospect Quay to enter Wandsworth Park.

WANDSWORTH PARK opened in 1903 on the remains of North Field which had an old riverside path. Across the river is Hurlingham House built in 1760 and now Hurlingham Club where the first polo match was played in 1875.

At the far end of the park leave the river to go through an archway behind the houses and pass through Blade Mews into Deodar Road.

DEODAR ROAD has Putney's only riverside houses. Writer Edna O'Brien lived at number 87 and Radio 4 programme *Desert Island Discs* inventor Roy Plomley at 91. The road is crossed by the District Line bridge, opened in 1889, which has a pedestrian link to Putney Bridge Underground Station on the far bank.

The road turns left to the main road. Opposite is Park Lodge and almshouses. Go right past Brewhouse Street (leading to a drawdock) to Putney High Street and right to Putney Bridge.

Refreshments

Hay's Wharf: Horniman at Hay's. 10am-11pm. Sat & Sun 10am-6pm.

Southwark Cathedral: Pizza Express. Mon-Fri lunchtimes.

Southwark: Old Thameside Inn, St Mary Overy Wharf. 11am-9pm; weekends 12-4pm. Food until 7.30pm; weekends until 2.30pm.

Bankside: Founders Arms. 11am-11pm. (Sun 12-10.30pm.)

Lambeth Bridge: Museum of Garden History café. Open daily except Mon Mar-Nov 10.30am-4pm; Sun until 5pm.

Wandsworth Bridge: McDonalds. Open 24 hours.

Accommodation

City YHA, Carter Lane, EC4 (near St Paul's Cathedral) (0171 236 4965).

Transport

Tower Bridge: Underground to Tower Hill.

Vauxhall: Underground and rail (South West Trains).

Putney: Rail (South West Trains) or Underground from Putney Bridge (on left bank).

Map

OS Landranger 176 (West London).

Former teahouse at Syon Park

3. Putney to Kingston
13 miles

This section takes the Path out of urban London and past several fine riverside mansions and gardens including Kew Gardens. Putney is the start of the towpath which runs as far as Inglesham in Wiltshire and is used by the Thames Path for most of the way. Beyond Putney's boundary, marked by Beverley Brook, the environment is rural. Birds seen here include grey herons, coots and plenty of Canada Geese. Cormorants are common around Chiswick. At Teddington the river ceases to be tidal.

PUTNEY The landmark church tower is 15th-century. The church's Bishop West Chapel recalls the local baker's son who became Bishop of Ely and Catherine of Aragon's chaplain. Thomas Cromwell, who took Henry VIII's side and implemented the Reformation, was also local born. Later Thomas's relative Oliver Cromwell chaired the Putney Debates in the church - a plaque (south side) records this first public discussion of democratic principles which influenced the drafting of the US constitution. At this time the Roundheads threw a pontoon bridge across to Fulham. When the first permanent bridge was erected in 1729, running from behind the church, it was the only road crossing between Kingston and London Bridge. The present bridge dates from 1886. Historian Edward Gibbon was baptised in the church in 1737 and a century on Charles Dickens is thought to have had this building in mind when he described 'David Copperfield's wedding. Writer Lewis Carroll often stayed with his uncle at Park Lodge next to the almshouses in Putney Bridge Road.

From the south end of Putney Bridge walk upstream along Lower Richmond Road and turn on to the Embankment. Just before the pier there is a bollard marked UBR indicating the University Boat Race start. Continue past The Star & Garter and The Duke's Head to reach the rowing clubs and boathouses. (Behind trees opposite is Fulham Palace, the Bishop of London's residence from 1141 to 1973, where England's longest moat was fed by the river.) The road ends at Beverley Brook.

BEVERLEY BROOK flows down from Richmond Park to serve here as the Wandsworth-Richmond borough boundary - once the London-Surrey border. Here, in the creek mouth, Putney's rubbish was tipped into barges to go down the Thames. Almost opposite is Fulham football ground known as 'Craven Cottage' after a picturesque riverside villa which stood on the site from 1780 until burnt down in 1888.

At once the towpath has a rural feel as it passes the bushes and old ash trees alongside Barn Elms playing fields. Beyond the Queen Elizabeth Walk turning, the towpath runs below Barn Elms Wetlands where there is the Boat Race mile post.

BARN ELMS The playing fields to the south were the grounds of a mansion owned by Sir Francis Walsingham who often entertained Elizabeth I. The Wetlands was created in the mid 1990s out of the former Barn Elms Reservoir.

Just before passing Harrods Depository there is a view of Thames Wharf.

THAMES WHARF was Duckham's oil depot. The wharf's canteen became the River Café in 1987 and was soon *The Times* Italian Restaurant of the Year and said to serve better Italian food than many restaurants in Italy. Architect Richard Rogers occupies offices and studios here.

HARRODS VILLAGE is a late 1990s development on a site purchased by Harrods in 1893 as a depository for the storage of furniture and possessions by those taking up postings in the Empire. Families returning home would store their furniture here and live in a Harrods flat at the back of the Knightsbridge store whilst looking for a permanent home. The main Harrods Depository building on the riverside, completed in 1914, is a familiar landmark on the Boat Race course but its similar silhouette to the Brompton Road store causes confusion in the minds of some television viewers when the commentator speaks of crews "passing Harrods". Immediately behind is The Charles Harrod Building, a former soap factory and the original depository. The Richard Burbidge Building was a candle factory.

Beyond here there is a view of Poly Gram on Chancellors Wharf just downstream of the Riverside Studios.

CHANCELLORS WHARF Poly Gram is on the site of Brandenburgh House where Queen Caroline lived during George IV's attempts to divorce her. Watermen took the Queen's side and held a massive demonstration of support here on the water. The Queen died at the house in 1821 just a year after being refused entry to her husband George IV's coronation. The following year the mansion was demolished.

Pass under Hammersmith Bridge.

HAMMERSMITH BRIDGE The first suspension bridge was built in the 1820s by William Tierney Clark who went on to build Marlow Bridge and is buried in St Paul's Hammersmith where the memorial stone bears the outline of a bridge. The first bridge is seen in Walter Greaves' painting *Hammersmith Bridge on Boat Race Day*. The present bridge was erected in 1883-7 using the original piers and abutments.

Soon there is a view across to Hammersmith Pier.

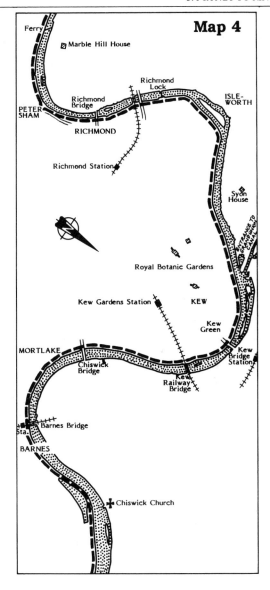

Map 4

Ferry

Marble Hill House

Richmond
Lock

Richmond
Bridge

ISLE-
WORTH

PETER
SHAM

RICHMOND

Richmond Station

Syon
House

ENTRANCE TO
GRAND UNION CANAL

Royal Botanic Gardens

Kew Gardens Station

KEW

Kew
Green

MORTLAKE

Kew
Bridge
Station

Chiswick
Bridge

Kew
Railway
Bridge

Barnes Bridge

Sta.

BARNES

Chiswick Church

HAMMERSMITH PIER marks a filled in creek. Alongside is The Dove - a 17th-century coffee house turned pub featured in A.P. Herbert's novel *The Water Gypsies*. Just upstream is the four storey Kelmscott House, home of William Morris whose country house was riverside Kelmscott Manor. In August 1880 he took a week sailing upstream to his second home.

The towpath bends south past St Paul's School grounds to draw level with Chiswick across the water.

CHISWICK is partly hidden by the Eyot planted with willows once cut to make fish baskets. Just visible behind the upstream end is Fuller's brewery which used to land hops and malt by barge. Fishermen lived in cottages near the Church Drawdock which had a ferry until 1934. Artist William Hogarth is buried in front of the church and James Whistler is in the cemetery. Upstream is residential Church Wharf, once occupied by Thornycroft shipbuilding which moved to Southampton in 1904 when destroyers became too large to pass under bridges, and Corney Reach (with pier) on the site of Corney House visited by Elizabeth I in 1602.

The towpath is alongside the Leg O'Mutton nature reserve before merging with the road at Barnes.

BARNES CHURCH, rebuilt after the 1978 fire in which the 16th-century tower survived with the clock in working order, was consecrated by Archbishop Langton on his way back from securing King John's assent to Magna Carta at Runnymede. Opposite the pond is Milbourne House where novelist Henry Fielding lived - the Georgian facade hides an Elizabethan building. Composer Gustav Holst lived at 10 The Terrace (by the river) where he wrote his *Planet Suite* in the main bedroom. The railway bridge dates from 1846 with the footbridge attached in 1895 strong enough to hold a Boat Race crowd.

Where the road leaves the river continue on the towpath behind Ye White Hart and along the back of Mortlake, passing The Limes and the brewery by the drawdock to The Ship at Thames Bank.

MORTLAKE is famous for its tapestries, including those now at

Hampton Court, made here from 1619 to 1703 by Flemish weavers. Now Watney's on the site continues the brewery association begun last century when hops and coal arrived by barge. The much restored church retains its Tudor tower - the bells were rung whenever Elizabeth I passed on the river between London and Richmond. The Ship was once the Boat Race finishing point. J.M.W.Turner painted two views of the Thames from The Limes' garden. Chiswick Bridge was built in 1933.

Pass the Boat Race finishing post to go under the bridge. For the next mile the path is rural with a view of Grove Park backgardens (right) and the Public Record Office (left) before passing under Kew Railway Bridge. Beyond Oliver's Ait is a view of Strand-on-the-Green.

STRAND-ON-THE-GREEN was a cluster of fishermen's cottages until the 1770s. Painter John Zoffany lived at Zoffany House (the blue plaque can just be seen) from 1780 to 1810 and in his *Last Supper* he modelled the Apostles on local fishermen and Judas on a churchwarden at Kew - so the painting has ended up in St Paul's Brentford rather than Kew Church. The house was recently the home of television writer Carla Lane. The bridge carrying the District Line opened in 1869.

Pass under Kew Bridge to reach Kew.

KEW BRIDGE was re-named Edward VII Bridge when the present structure was opened by the King in 1903 but the original name first used in 1759 has stuck. The main road runs across the Green with its church where the late Queen Mary's parents married after her father proposed in the Gardens. The mausoleum at the east end held the remains (now at Windsor) of her grandparents, the Duke and Duchess of Cambridge, who lived at Cambridge Cottage. Painter George Gainsborough is buried outside the Church's south wall whilst Zoffany is on the east side. In Kew Road The Maids of Honour teashop bakes cakes to a secret recipe used for Henry VIII. On the far bank is the 1867 tower of a pumping station (now Kew Bridge Steam Museum) which had river water pumped up it to run down into the mains.

Whilst passing the back of Kew Green the river is divided by islands.

BRENTFORD AIT (*ait* means a small river island) was planted with trees in the 1920s to screen Brentford's gasworks. In the gap (known as Hog Hole) between the two islands can be seen St George's Brentford (now the Musical Museum). The third island is a former osier ground where barges were repaired until 1980.

Inland is Kew Palace and Kew Gardens.

KEW PALACE, built in Dutch style in 1631, is the smallest Royal palace. George III spent his last years here when the garden was subject to flooding. Queen Victoria's parents were married in the drawing room which has several Zoffany portraits. (Open to public via Gardens.)

KEW GARDENS, the Royal Botanic Gardens, was founded in 1759 by Princess Augusta whose greenhouse is now the Orangery. Her landmark pagoda was decorated with dragons until the Prince Regent pawned them to pay debts. The Aroid House once stood at the back of Buckingham Palace as its twin still does. Entry via Brentford Ferry Gate - the ferry ceased operation in 1939. Open 9.30am-6pm (dusk in winter); admission charge.

There is a view across the river to Brentford before Syon House comes into view across the north bank meadows.

BRENTFORD During the 17th century bricks, fruit and fish went to London by barges which returned with horse dung ballast used as fertiliser - there was a Dung Wharf. The River Brent (Grand Union Canal) joins here. Just upstream is Brentford Dock which was completed in 1859 and closed in 1964.

SYON HOUSE, home of the Duke of Northumberland whose lion crest can be seen on the roof, was a convent until the Reformation. The sisters survived abroad and are now in Devon. Lady Jane Grey made her bid to oust Mary I from here and Charles I, whilst a prisoner at Hampton Court, came by water to see his children. In 1616 Pocahontas, who found London rather dirty, was loaned the country house. The tide meadow and its natural creeks are washed twice daily by freshwater pushed back by the tide. In 1642 the Battle of Brentford was fought to the north when Royalists took the town, slashing fishing nets and driving defenders into the Thames. The Civil War might have ended by agreement the next day at Turnham Green but for the sound of an ammunition barge being blown up here by Royalists, which was mistaken for gunfire.

At the far end of the estate is Isleworth village.

ISLEWORTH The church is modern but retains its 15th-century tower. Bodies of Great Plague victims were brought here by barge and buried behind the church. The 500 year old London Apprentice pub recalls the apprentices who rowed up from the City on their annual day off. Today many Westminster politicians come here by road to The Ferry House, where Turner lived, for Lord Gilmour's annual garden party described as "the Goodwood of the political season" and once causing a government's Commons vote to fall to just four. The downstream white residence is a Tudor boathouse converted during the Georgian period into a teahouse. The ferry, restored in 1995 after a 32 year gap which had seen an attempted revival in 1983 fail, operates at weekends 10am-6pm Jun-Sept; small charge.

Stay on the towpath alongside the tree-lined Old Deer Park with modern Isleworth hidden by Isleworth Ait. On turning south-east there is Richmond Half-Tide Weir and the first lock (which saves Richmond from a dramatic drop in water level at low tide). Beyond two bridges is Richmond's first house.

RICHMOND-UPON-THAMES was West Sheen until Henry VII called his palace here after his earldom derived from Yorkshire's Richmond. Mary I and Philip of Spain honeymooned here and Elizabeth I died here. The gatehouse and courtyard can be found off Water Lane. Maids of Honour Row was built in 1724 for the Princess of Wales' ladies-in-waiting but the last monarch to live here was Charles I whose chaplain founded the almshouses in The Vineyard. Actor Edmund Kean is buried in the church having had his body refused by Westminster Abbey due to a drunken reputation. A plaque in Paradise Street marks the house where Leonard and Virginia Woolf started the Hogarth Press on the kitchen table. Richmond Bridge was built in 1777 when it cost $^{1}/2$d to cross and 1d if pushing a wheelbarrow. The neo-classical development next to the bridge is by Quinlan Terry. The former 1891 Jesus College

Oxford barge was moored here in 1993 to be a restaurant.

Pass under the bridge to Richmond Landing Stage where the Captain Webb floating hotel is often moored. When the towpath reaches a gate leading to Petersham Meadows bear right to stay by the river and pass Glover's Island. Soon River Lane runs down from Petersham village.

PETERSHAM The church across the meadows is partly Norman and has box pews. Weddings here have included Prince Rupert in 1664 and the Queen Mother's parents in 1881. George Vancouver, who discovered Vancouver Island and lived at River Lane's Navigator's Cottage, is buried by the churchyard's south wall. Cows grazing on the meadows are the nearest to central London.

After 400 yards Marble Hill House can be seen on the far bank.

MARBLE HILL HOUSE was completed in 1729 for George II's mistress Lady Suffolk and in 1795 Mrs Fitzherbert, the Prince Regent's first wife, lived there. Hammerton's Ferry, which can be hailed from the steps, was started in 1909 by Walter Hammerton. Third owner Stan Rust operates an electric Peace of Mind ferry (built in 1997 at Teddington) at weekends 10am-6.30pm (or dusk if earlier) and daily Feb-Oct 10am-6pm; small charge.

Soon there is Ham House behind the trees on the towpath side.

HAM HOUSE, built in 1610, is little changed since the Earl of Lauderdale (the L in Charles II's Cabal) and his wife made it their home after marrying at Petersham Church. Soon after John Evelyn wrote that Ham "is indeed inferior to few of the best villas in Italy itself; the House furnished like a great Prince's; the Park with Flower Gardens, Orangeries, Groves, Avenues, Courts, Statues, Perspectives, Fountains, Aviaries and all this on the banks of the sweetest river in the World...". The garden, open daily, is a rare survival of the formal 17th-century style. Ham House is in the care of the National Trust which encourages visitors to arrive either on foot or by boat as in the 17th century. Ham House is open Easter-Oct; Mon-Wed 1-5pm; weekends 12-5pm; admission charge. The garden is open daily except Fri; admission free.

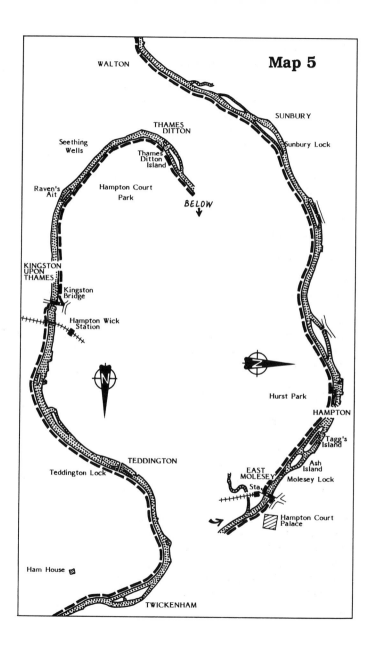

Map 5

WALTON

SUNBURY

THAMES
DITTON

Sunbury Lock

Seething
Wells

Thames
Ditton
Island

Raven's
Ait

Hampton Court
Park

BELOW

KINGSTON
UPON
THAMES

Kingston
Bridge

Hampton Wick
Station

N

N

Hurst Park

HAMPTON

Tagg's
Island

TEDDINGTON

Ash
Island

Teddington Lock

EAST
MOLESEY

Molesey Lock

Sta.

Hampton Court
Palace

Ham House

TWICKENHAM

Soon there is Eel Pie Island blocking the view of Twickenham.

EEL PIE ISLAND, once Twickenham Ayte, is named after a dish served on the island from the 16th century, sampled by Henry VIII and later served at the now demolished Eel Pie Island Hotel which opened in 1830. The 2 acre island was a well known picnic spot featured by Charles Dickens in *Nicholas Nickleby* where he writes of "a cold collation, bottled beer, shrub, and shrimp and to dance in the open air to the music of a locomotive band". In the Sixties the Hotel was popular for its pop concerts featuring the Rolling Stones. Today's 300 residents include a community of artists and Trevor Bayliss who lives in the self-built house where he invented the clockwork radio. Before the move to plastic, the University Boat Race boats were made in the boatyard on the north side. The island was served by ferry until 1956 when the toll bridge (2d until decimalization) linked to the Twickenham bank was built.

TWICKENHAM Alexander Pope, who lived in a riverside house (demolished), is buried in the church which has a 14th-century tower. The Vicarage was once home of tea merchant Thomas Twining. In 1958 the CND symbol was designed by local resident Gerald Holtom for the Aldermaston March. Upstream of the island, as the river begins to bend, there is a view of the former convent which includes Pope's Grotto where the poet entertained satirist Jonathan Swift.

The river turns south and between a dock entrance and Teddington there is the Boundary Stone.

THE BOUNDARY STONE marks the division between the downstream Port of London Authority and the Environment Agency (formerly Thames Conservancy) which is the controlling authority for upstream navigation.

TEDDINGTON The tidal Thames ends at the lock which takes its name from the village on the far bank reached by a long footbridge. The parish church dates from the 16th century but the landmark is St Alban's, known as 'The Thames Valley Cathedral' and based on Clermont-Ferrand Cathedral after the vicar visiting with a churchwarden exclaimed: "If only we could have a church like that!" Built in 1887-9 it had Fr Alfred Hope Patten, who restored the Shrine of Our Lady at Walsingham, as curate, and playwright Noel Coward, born at 131 Waldegrave Road, in the choir. The huge church was declared redundant in 1977. R.D. Blackmore wrote *Launa Doone* in the 1860s whilst living on the site of Doone Close. By the river is the former Warner Brothers film studios used now for television programmes. Teddington is also the end of the dual Thames Path route which begins at the Greenwich foot tunnel.

Soon there is a view on the Teddington bank down Broom Water.

BROOM WATER was a natural creek extended three times its length in 1863 as a waterside housing development.

The towpath later joins a riverside road before running under a long line of trees on the edge of Canbury Gardens.

CANBURY GARDENS was marshland known as The Eyots until the dumping of building waste led to draining for a park in 1889. However, the promenade became known as 'Perfume Parade' due to smells from a fertiliser factory. Immediately to the south between 1947 and 1994 the riverside landmark was Kingston Power Station.

Go under a railway bridge, past Turk's boats landing stage and under Kingston Bridge to reach the town.

Refreshments

Kew: Maids of Honour teashop, Kew Road. Until 5.30pm but closed all day Sun and Mon from after lunch.

Kew: St Anne's Church, Kew Green. Teas on summer Sun afternoons until 5.45pm.

Ham House: Coffee, lunches & teas in Orangery 11am-5.30pm except Thu & Fri Easter-Oct. Open winter weekends except Jan-Feb.

Teddington: Peg Woffington Cottage Tearoom near church. Teas weekends 3.30-6pm. Closed Bank Holidays.

Accommodation

Richmond: 4 Church Road, TW9 2QA (0181 948 5852).

Richmond: 37 Church Rd, TW9 9UA (0181 940 5237).

Transport

Putney: Underground to Putney Bridge (on left bank) or rail (South West Trains) to Putney.

Kew Bridge: Underground and rail (Silverlink Metro) from Kew Gardens or rail (South West Trains) from Kew Bridge (left bank).

Richmond: Underground and Rail (South West Trains and Silverlink Metro).

Kingston: Rail (South West Trains).

Tourist Information

Richmond: Old Town Hall (0181 940 9125).

Map

OS Landranger 176 (West London).

Hampton Court Bridge from East Molesey bank

4. Kingston to Chertsey
11 miles

At Kingston the towpath crosses to the left bank for the first time. Beyond Hampton Court, on the edge of the county of London, the towpath switches back to the right bank as far as Shepperton where mink, which attack young swans, may be encountered. Walkers should note that the last ferry at Shepperton is at 5.30pm (6.30pm May-Aug). An alternative waymarked route, handy for those wishing to use Shepperton Station, can be followed across Walton Bridge.

KINGSTON-UPON-THAMES King Alfred chose to be crowned here in an attempt to unite Mercia (left bank) with the Saxons against the Danes who later came up river. Six Saxon kings including Ethelred the Unready were crowned on the Coronation Stone outside the Guildhall. The Roman ford was replaced with a bridge by the 12th century. The church has a 14th-century pillar painting of St Blaise (patron of local drapers) and Holy Trinity Chapel built by the Shipmen's Guild (now Trinity House). The church was the setting for John Millais' 1863 painting *My First Sermon* and its sequel showing a little girl asleep. Lloyd's Bank has a plaque to HMV dog Nipper who is buried on the site. The market operates under a Charles I charter which allows no other within a 7 mile radius. The riverside Bishop out of Residence pub is on the site of a house used in the 14th century by Bishop of Winchester William of Wykeham when travelling between Winchester and Southwark.

Cross Kingston Bridge and turn left down Barge Walk to reach the riverbank. Opposite, beyond the Bishop out of Residence, can be seen Hogsmill River which rises near Epsom. After ½ mile, and before the 1850 Italianate tower of St Raphael's Church on the far bank, there is a view of Turk's boatyard.

TURK'S BOATYARD moved in 1996 from below Kingston Bridge to this site where Royal Waterman Mike Turk's ancestor kept a salmon weir for Henry VIII.

The river curves south-west to Raven's Ait.

RAVEN'S AIT, an island residential watersport centre, was largely an osier ground in the 19th century. The name derivation is uncertain but Seething Wells on the far bank recalls therapeutic springs there. Hart's Ferry operates upstream of the island on Sundays.

The Path continues alongside Hampton Court Park with views of residential Seething Wells and Thames Ditton on the far bank.

THAMES DITTON ISLAND is now covered by 48 timber houses and bungalows. The village on the right bank behind has a 13th-century church and a riverside inn, The Olde Swan, dating from the same period.

Here by the towpath is The Pavilion.

THE PAVILION, designed by Wren and built in 1700 for William III's entertaining, has been the home of Queen Victoria's father and more recently the late Cecil King.

As the path comes level with Hampton Court Palace's Privy

Garden there is a view across to the confluence with the River Mole which rises near Gatwick Airport.

HAMPTON COURT PALACE was a Knights Hospitaller house rebuilt by Cardinal Wolsey to such a size that he needed almost 500 servants. He gave his residence to Henry VIII who brought five of his six wives here - he is said to have been in the tennis court when he heard confirmation of Anne Boleyn's execution downstream at the Tower of London. His daughter Elizabeth I usually spent Christmas here. To the Tudors and Stuarts the river was the main highway and Charles II was given two gondolas with four gondoliers from Venice for use here. The Vine, the world's oldest and largest with roots watered by the Thames, was planted in 1765 for George III who never lived here. His son William IV started guided tours and Queen Victoria opened the main rooms for free public viewing. Today the Palace is open daily; admission charge.

Walk over Hampton Court Bridge (using handy roadcrossing to the right first) to reach East Molesey.

HAMPTON COURT BRIDGE The first bridge built in 1753 was Chinese in appearance having been inspired by the new bridge at Walton. The toll for walkers ($^1/_2$d on weekdays and 1d on Sundays) continued in force for two more structures until 1876. The tollhouse can be seen as part of The Mitre Hotel which, along with the 1865 cast iron bridge, features in several Alfred Sisley paintings. The castellated abutments of this crossing remain just upstream of its successor designed by Edwin Lutyens and opened in 1933.

EAST MOLESEY Bridge Street indicates the line of the old main road before the bridge was realigned. When St Mary's Church was rebuilt in the 1860s old toll bridge posts were placed at the churchyard entrance to deter body-snatchers who came by river hoping to sell to London medical schools. The Bell, near the church, has 'circa 1450' above the door. The railway station is now called Hampton Court.

Continue upstream along River Bank to a bus stop where a slope leads on to the towpath. Beyond Molesey Lock and weir there are Ash and Tagg's Islands with a Swiss cottage seen between the two.

TAGG'S ISLAND, once Walnut Tree Island, is named after Royal Waterman Tom Tagg who ran a boatyard and hotel here in the 19th century. Later Fred Karno covered the island with his leisure complex. The Swiss cottage on the Hampton bank was brought from Switzerland in 1899.

Later the towpath has a rough surface as it heads towards the former Hurst Park Racecourse opposite Hampton Church.

HAMPTON The riverside church, completed in 1831 with all materials delivered by barge, contains work by *Radio Times* illustrator Eric Fraser who lived next to the churchyard in the house of Edward VI's childhood nurse. Garrick's Temple was built in 1755 for actor Richard Garrick who lived in the house behind. Zoffany visited in 1762 and painted Garrick and his wife at the white Garrick's Temple dedicated to Shakespeare. The ferry has been operating since at least 1519. Hurst Park Racecourse, on the towpath side, closed in 1960.

The long Platt's Eyot (where torpedo boats were built) screens a waterworks. Beyond the island the rising towpath passes riverside homes. At a bend the way is below a long wall, hiding reservoirs, where sheep may be spotted. On coming level with Grand Junction Island the path passes between wartime defences. After a mile the wall gives way to railings and across the water Sunbury Court is seen behind Sunbury Court Island. When level with the end of the island there is a City of London post (indicating that coal brought into London is subject to tax) on the West Molesey-Walton parish boundary. Soon Sunbury on the far bank comes into view.

SUNBURY-ON-THAMES Most of the village is unseen apart from a pub and former boat builders. Sunbury Court, now the Salvation Army Youth Centre, was built in about 1770 as a riverside mansion. Just below Sunbury Lock in the late 18th century was one of several paygates for the towing horses - 3d here but only 2d at Laleham. Behind the lock island is the church and Monksbridge, an 18th-century house where the future Edward VIII often stayed enjoying swimming and boating as guest of the Dudley Ward family.

After the weir the towpath is along the Walton Mile - an almost straight course used for regattas. The second island is Wheatley's Ait.

WHEATLEY'S AIT was an osier ground until the 1880s. The first residents were a group of bachelors who came at weekends and holidays. Later they allowed women to join them so long as they left by midnight. Now it is a second home to 16 families.

Just before a bridge there is The Anglers Tavern on Walton Wharf at Walton-on-Thames.

WALTON WHARF is a former ferry point with the grass approach seen opposite. As early as Tudor times timber was sent to London from here. In the 19th century coal was unloaded for the gas company. Livestock often watered here included the occasional circus elephant. At the top of the slope round the corner is The Old Manor House pub said to have been the home of Judge George Jeffreys. The nearby Swan is where in 1910 songwriter Jerome Kern met his wife Eva who was the landlord's daughter. Composer Sir Arthur Sullivan lived at River House between 1894 and 1898.

Cross the backwater and continue round the double bend to Walton Bridge.

WALTON BRIDGE is the least attractive on the river being a temporary Bailey Bridge erected in 1953 (on the downstream side of the original crossing) following war damage. The first in 1750 was an unusual wooden geometrical design which appears in a Giovanni Canaletto painting. The second opened in 1783 and was painted by J.M.W.Turner. This is the site of a ford crossed by Julius Caesar in 64BC. The Walton (right) bank is known as Cowey Sale ('cow way') and at the back of the low lying meadow is the Engine River which was probably an earlier Thames channel on the flood plain. The Engine, rather than the Thames, is the former Middlesex-Surrey boundary and today the boundary between Spelthorne and Elmbridge District Councils.

(Walkers should note that the final ferry at Shepperton is at 5.30pm; May-Aug 6.30pm. The alternative waymarked route to Shepperton is over Walton Bridge.)

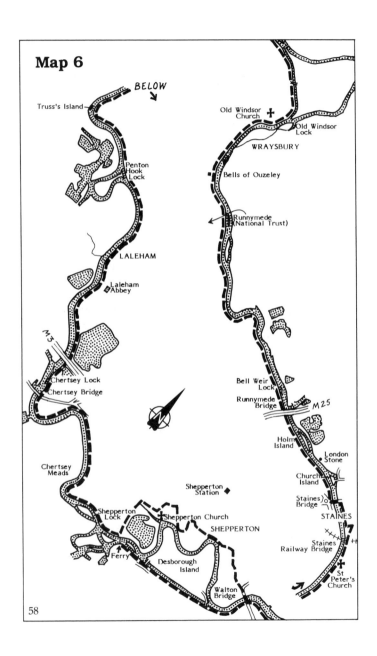

Map 6

BELOW ↓

Truss's Island

Penton Hook Lock

LALEHAM

Laleham Abbey

M3

Chertsey Lock

Chertsey Bridge

Chertsey Meads

Shepperton Lock

Ferry

Shepperton Church

SHEPPERTON

Shepperton Station

Desborough Island

Walton Bridge

Old Windsor Church

Old Windsor Lock

WRAYSBURY

Bells of Ouzeley

Runnymede (National Trust)

Bell Weir Lock

Runnymede Bridge

M 25

Holm Island

London Stone

Church Island

Staines Bridge

STAINES

Staines Railway Bridge

St Peter's Church

Before the next bridge the river divides giving navigation and walkers the choice between the old channel and the man-made cut under the bridge.

DESBOROUGH CUT Over a century after the cut was first suggested (and supported by the Grand Old Duke of York living nearby at Weybridge) work began in 1930. The ³/₄ mile channel, avoiding five tortuous bends, was opened in 1935 by Lord Desborough, Thames Conservancy Board Chairman. Desborough Island, created by the cut, still has the old towpath which gives views of Shepperton Manor and Church.

The Thames Path follows the cut ahead. Beyond the second Desborough Island bridge the Old and New Thames merge and the towpath is soon level with D'Oyly Carte Island.

D'OYLY CARTE ISLAND was Folly or Silly Eyot until theatre manager Richard D'Oyly Carte decided in about 1890 to build Eyot House on the island which had become more substantial following dredging. It was to have been the summer annex to The Savoy Hotel but when a drinks licence was refused the house became D'Oyly Carte's home. Visitors included William S. Gilbert and Sir Arthur Sullivan - willow trees at nearby Shepperton inspired the *Mikado* song *Tit-willow*. Before the bridge was built visitors called a boat by ringing the bell at the lychgate on the path.

The towpath crosses the river at the ferry leaving a riverside path to continue into Weybridge. Ring the bell on the hour to call the ferryboat from the far bank.

SHEPPERTON FERRY reopened in 1986 after a 26 year break. There has been a ferry here since Henry VI's reign. In the 1700s it cost 1s. to take a drove of oxon across for Kingston Market. Between the World Wars, when Sid Kingman was ferryman for 22 years, the passenger fare was 1d. or 2d. for cyclists and the service operated daily 6am-10pm. Today the ferry runs at least every hour 8.30am-5pm with a final run at 5.30pm (May-Aug 6.30pm); small charge. Ferry information 01932 254844.

The ferry lands at Ferry Lane on the edge of Shepperton. Turn left along the road to pass Shepperton Lock. Round the first bend

there is Thames Court pub-restaurant just before Pharaoh's Island.

PHARAOH'S ISLAND The name dates from the Battle of the Nile when the island was given to Lord Nelson. The present 23 properties tend to have Egyptian names such as Ramses, Sphinx and Thebes. Past residents include actor Ian Hendry.

Here the river has houses on both banks. When the road moves away from the bank the towpath is on grass with only the occasional house. Later when the way narrows there may be several houseboats. At a kissing gate the towpath is on the edge of Dumpsey Mead - a sea of yellow ragwort in summer - where cattle water at the river. Soon there is a view of Chertsey Bridge beyond the bend.

Refreshments

Walton-on-Thames: The Swan. 11am-11pm. (Sun 12-10.30pm.) Food until 2.30pm 7-9pm.

Shepperton Lock: Teas and ices in summer.

Shepperton Lock: Thames Court is just upstream from lock. 11am-11pm. (Sun 12-10.30pm. Meals, children's menu.

Accommodation

Kingston: 1 Riverside Close, KT1 2JG (0181 546 5828).

Kingston: 281A Richmond Road, KT2 5DJ (0181 546 7389).

East Molesey: Meadowcroft, 3 Spencer Rd, KT8 0SP (0181 783 1426).

Transport

Kingston: Rail (South West Trains).

Shepperton: Rail (South West Trains).

Chertsey: Rail (South West Trains).

Tourist Information

Kingston: The Market House, The Market Place (0181 547 5594).

Map

OS Landranger 176 (West London).

> ## *Alternative Route to Shepperton avoiding ferry*

Cross Walton Bridge to Windmill Green and at once bear half left into Walton Lane. As the road bears sharp left keep ahead down the side of a wall (left) by a playing field. At Lower Halliford's green go left. Ahead is Peacock House marked by a blue plaque.

PEACOCK HOUSE The riverside house was bought in 1826 by Thomas Love Peacock, author of the poem *The Genius of the Thames*, for his mother and it became his own home until his death in 1866. His son-in-law novelist George Meredith lived in Vine Cottage across the green.

Cross Walton Lane and bear right on the path past the river viewpoint. Go left into Russell Road to pass The Red Lion and The Ship Hotel. When the narrow pavement ends take the path by the backwater on the left. The path soon rejoins the road. (To reach Shepperton Station continue ahead and go right at the roundabout to walk up the main shopping street.) The Thames Path turns left over a footbridge and right to continue parallel to the road. At a junction go left up the approach to Shepperton Cricket Club. Just before the cricket ground go left at a gate to find a path which leads to the riverside. Here there is a fine view of Shepperton Manor.

SHEPPERTON means 'shepherds' habitation' and according to Domesday Book belonged to Westminster Abbey. The church was destroyed by flooding during the winter of 1605-6 when the Thames was still tidal here. The present church was built in 1613 with the tower added in the next century. Behind is the Rectory which when new, in Henry VII's reign, was often visited by the Dutch theologian Desiderius Erasmus who was a friend of the Rector. George Eliot wrote *Scenes from Clerical Life* at Shepperton Manor.

Walk upstream and follow the manor grounds wall to reach Church Road. Go left to pass Church Square (left) and continue into Chertsey Road. Go left down Ferry Lane to Shepperton Lock.

Truss's Island stone

5. Chertsey to Staines
4 miles

This short section is on the left bank through countryside which has long been a centre for riverside residences and holiday homes. Although only 4 miles long there are two locks.

CHERTSEY BRIDGE The first was built in 1410 and maintained by Chertsey Abbey. The present bridge, a little upstream, was completed in 1785. In the mid 18th century Chertsey cricket team met at The Cricketers on the town bank. Charles Dickens features the bridge in *Oliver Twist*.

CHERTSEY, $^1/2$ mile from the bridge, was called "the stillest of towns" by poet Matthew Arnold. The Thames braid from Penton Hook to just above Chertsey Bridge was probably man-made for Chertsey Abbey which lay behind the parish church. When Henry VI was murdered in the Tower his body (after being exposed at St Paul's) was brought by barge to the Abbey but his tomb became such an object of pilgrimage that after 22 years the coffin was moved further upstream to Windsor. At the Dissolution in 1537 the Benedictine community moved to Bisham whilst buildings here were demolished and the stone taken downstream to improve Hampton Court. In 1540 the Abbey church's steeple stone went to Weybridge to enlarge a house for the divorced Anne of Cleves. The library and orchard followed on barges. But there was still enough accommodation left in 1548 for Archbishop Cranmer to hold meetings about the first *Book of Common Prayer*. An abbey bell, now in the church, is rung as a curfew at 8pm between Michaelmas and Lady Day. When poet Abraham Cowley died here in 1667 his body was taken by river for burial in Westminster Abbey. Chertsey Museum in Windsor Street is open Tue-Fri 12.30-4.30pm; Sat 11am-4pm; admission free.

The towpath does not cross Chertsey Bridge to the town side but continues along a road until past Chertsey Lock. Just beyond the weir there is a view (left) of Chertsey Church tower. After passing under the M3 the path is more substantial almost as far as Laleham Park. Laleham House is behind Burway Rowing Club. The nearby main road eventually turns inland at Ferry Lane to Laleham.

LALEHAM means 'village by willows'. Laleham House was home of the Lucan family who remain landowners. The missing Earl is golf club president and patron of the church where there is a Lucan Chapel. Churchyard tombs include Lord Lucan of Charge of the Light Brigade fame (east side). Matthew Arnold, buried opposite the south small door, was born at Ferry Lane's Muncaster House where his famous father Thomas ran a school. The ferry, run by a

Lucan tenant in Ferry House on the far bank until the late 1970s, provided a short cut to Chertsey.

Soon the towpath passes Blacksmith Lane linking the towpath with the village. The towpath again joins a road and, after crossing the Queen Mary Reservoir water intake, reaches Penton Hook.

PENTON HOOK Here the river takes $^{1}/_{2}$ mile to travel 20 yards. The lock opened in 1815 saving the loop although before this barges often broke through the narrow neck. This was the highest of the locks controlled by the City of London whose arms are seen on the lock cottages.

There are now residences on both sides as far as Staines. On approaching a bend the path unusually does not stay by the water but hugs the houses before turning north with the Thames. On the far side is Truss's Island.

TRUSS'S ISLAND, restored in 1992 with water again on all sides, is named after the City of London's Navigation Clerk of Works Charles Truss. The stone, bearing the Corporation shield and the island's name, was placed in the centre in 1804 but has the date 1774 which is the year of his appointment. The City, then responsible for the Thames as far as Staines, had allowed the river to become so obstructed and towpaths so eroded that it was in danger of losing its ancient rights. Truss spent 36 years restoring the river which saw a huge increase in traffic with the opening of the Thames & Severn Canal.

After $^{1}/_{2}$ mile there is St Peter's Church.

ST PETER'S, opened in 1894 after the arrival of the railway caused Staines to expand south, was financed by Sir Edward Clarke KC who offered to pay for a church if a neighbour bought the gates. The following year he defended Oscar Wilde at his trial. The site was chosen by Lady Clarke who had seen a church on the banks of Devon's River Dart and Sir Edward moved swiftly when riverside elms were threatened by a builder. Then the couple lived a little

Oakley Court

Boulter's Lock
College barge passing Medmenham Abbey

downstream in a house with eight acres of garden by the towpath but later Sir Edward sold it to Indian cricketer Rangi Singh and built for himself the house next to the church which is now the Vicarage. On Rogation Sunday the St Peter's congregation assemble on the towpath for the blessing of the river.

Ahead is Staines Railway Bridge where the towpath, but not the Thames Path, switches banks.

STAINES RAILWAY BRIDGE, built in 1856 for the Staines-Reading line, was painted with yellow stripes in 1995 to stop swans from flying into it. This point, where the towpath switches banks, was known as Shooting Off and the early 19th-century cottages immediately upstream of the bridge are called Hook On and Shoot Off as this was where barges were poled across to the towpath on the right bank whilst the horses were taken through the town to the bridge. Coming downstream the barge floated over with the current from the far side.

Follow the road past the cottages and The Pack Horse. Immediately beyond Thames Lodge Hotel turn left to return to the river. The Thames Path passes the back of Staines' Market Hall and crosses the entrance to the River Colne (which rises at Colney Heath near Hatfield) to reach Staines Bridge. Go under the bridge and at once right to reach steps leading up to the road.

Refreshments

Chertsey: Catered 4 Coffee Shop, Guildford Street. Coffee, teas and snacks including takeaway. 8am-5pm except Sun.

Near Staines: St Peter's Church by towpath. Teas on lawn on summer Sun 3-5pm.

Accommodation

Chertsey Bridge: Camping & Caravanning Club site, Bridge Road (01932 562405 before 8pm). Open all year. Non-members welcome. Go over bridge from towpath and turn right to find site on riverbank opposite lock.

Laleham: Camping Club site, Laleham Park (01932 564149). Apr-Sep. Near river to south of village.

Transport

Chertsey: Rail (South West Trains).

Staines: Rail (South West Trains).

Tourist Information

Spelthorne Council Office, Knowle Green, Staines, TW18 1XB (01784 451499).

Map

OS Landranger 176 (West London).

6. Staines to Windsor

7¹/₂ miles

Here the towpath passes from Surrey into the Royal County of Berkshire having first run along the side of Runnymede where Magna Carta was accepted by King John. Opposite Datchet, where the towpath in the Windsor Castle grounds is closed to walkers, the Crown Estate has provided new footpaths on the left bank for the Thames Path.

STAINES When the barons gathered here in 1215 to meet King John on Runnymede they had to ford the river. The first bridge was built seven years later and replaced at least four times before the present structure designed by John Rennie of London Bridge fame opened in 1832 a little upstream from the old crossing where the Market Hall now stands. In its predecessor in 1603 Sir Walter Raleigh was found guilty of treason - plague forced the trial out of London. The parish church's tower was built 30 years later but the landmark is the 1903 Ashley's Brewery, now The Maltings residences. The London Stone, originally just downstream of the bridge but now in the riverside park west of the church, marks the end of the City of London's river jurisdiction (1197-1857). It stands in a playground next to the County Ditch which was the Middlesex-Buckinghamshire boundary. The Lord Mayor made an annual visit to touch the stone with a sword. Staines was the end of the tidal Thames until 1812 when the downstream locks were built. The attractive houses downstream of the bridge and opposite the town date from around 1750.

Cross the bridge and bear right to join the river at the McVitie's building. A high bridge takes the towpath over an inlet opposite the end of Church Island. The London Stone is on the far bank behind a lone mobile home just beyond the island - level with the City coal tax post on the towpath. Beyond here much of the far bank is an island although this is not at first obvious.

HOLM ISLAND has one house dating from 1888 and enlarged in its centenary year. The long island hides a smaller Hollyhock Island which until the 1930s had a small house called The Nest alleged to be a hideaway for Edward VIII and Mrs Simpson.

As the island ends the path crosses an inlet and winds through woodland to pass under the M25. At once Colne Brook (a branch of the River Colne) enters on the far bank and ahead is Bell Weir Lock.

BELL WEIR LOCK, dating from 1817, is named after weir-keeper and ferryman Charlie Bell who opened The Angler's Rest Hotel here in the 18th century. Its successor, The Runnymede Hotel, has a Charlie Bell's café-bar.

There is a mile of riverside homes broken by Nicholes Boatyard specialising in steam craft. At the far end follow the curving bank south with a view over to the wooded grounds of the lost Ankerwycke Priory. Beyond a kissing gate the way is between the river and a road running the length of the Runnymede meadow.

RUNNYMEDE King John agreed to Magna Carta somewhere in this field in 1215. The barons' demands were probably approved by the king symbolically kissing Archbishop Langton rather than by a signing of the document which has been called "the first ground and chief cornerstone of the Common Law of England". It confirmed the Thames as a highway by declaring that "all fishweirs shall be entirely removed from the Thames". The monument on the west side was erected by the American Bar Association. Nearby is the John F. Kennedy Memorial and behind on Cooper's Hill can be seen the Commonwealth Air Forces Memorial. The left bank Magna Carta Island is claimed by some as the real site of the King's meeting with the barons. The 'island', joined to the far bank, was part of Ankerwycke Priory and its Benedictine nuns owned the weirs and fisheries between here and Old Windsor.

After Lily Pond Inlet there is a clear view of the Magna Carta Memorial (left) and Magna Carta Island. At the end of the meadow stay by the river to pass the two lodges (one is a tearoom) and the boatyard. There is a short stretch of quiet towpath before the way is metalled and joins a pavement by a road. The separate towpath is resumed just before the pub.

THE BELLS OF OUZELEY is a 1936 building now run by Harvester Inns. The spelling was 'Ouseley' when it was "the picturesque inn" described in Jerome J. Jerome's *Three Men in a Boat* written in 1888. The bells are believed to be those of Oxford's Osney Abbey which in 1538 were being spirited down the river by monks trying to save them from the hands of Henry VIII's agents. When the barges went aground here the bells were hidden in the oozing mud. They have never been found but the bells of Christ Church Oxford are claimed as those of Osney.

The path is in front of a new development and through a boatyard before a rough surface is resumed. There are houses on both banks and several gardens extend over the towpath. At Old Windsor the path divides.

OLD WINDSOR is where Edward the Confessor had a palace before William the Conqueror moved the Royal residence to the present Castle site 3 miles away. Here in 1072 a Synod agreed that the Archbishop of Canterbury should take precedence over York. The 13th-century church is unique in having the double dedication to St Peter and St Andrew. Near the churchyard's north-east gate there is the tomb of Mary Robinson who sat for artists Gainsborough, Romney and Reynolds.

Except to visit the church go right over the inlet. Soon there is a view of Honeypot Cottage on the far bank.

HONEYPOT COTTAGE, built in 1933 with local bricks and thatch, was the home of actress Beryl Reid from 1952 until her death in 1996. She was well known for taking in stray cats and at one time had 13 cats enjoying the round rooms. The square dining room was added by the actress whose ashes were scattered on the riverside garden.

Ahead is Friday Island and Old Windsor Lock.

FRIDAY ISLAND is so called because it is shaped like a footprint. There is a well and a small two bedroomed thatched cottage almost hidden by willows. For 25 years it was a second home for Dr Julius Grant, inventor of Marmite and secret agents' edible paper, who died in 1991 aged 89.

Beyond the lock the path is almost straight along the New Cut, built in 1822 to save a two bend detour. There is a first view of Windsor Castle ahead. After the Ham Island bridge the way is a rural path as far as Albert Bridge.

ALBERT BRIDGE and its upstream twin Victoria were designed by Prince Albert in 1851 as new crossings to Datchet. Until 1848 it was possible to continue here on the towpath along the side of Home Park attached to Windsor Castle. The Crown Estate, which also owns the left bank, has provided two new paths on each side of Datchet village for the Thames Path.

Climb the steps up on to Albert Bridge and cross the river. At once take a path on the right which runs down to a kissing gate and under the bridge to follow a riverside woodland path. On reaching a field (right) there is a view across the water to the buildings of Prince Consort's Home Farm. Later the path turns inland to avoid riverside gardens. On reaching a road do not go through the gate but turn left to walk along the side of another field. Pass through the two gates (opposite the entrance to Southlea Farm) and continue on the enclosed path to join the road. Turn left along the road to walk into Datchet and rejoin the river at the parish wharf by the High Street junction.

DATCHET Old Bridge House, at the river end of the short High Street, recalls the time when the High Street continued across the river and along a direct tree lined lane running through Home Park to Windsor. The road, featured in William Shakespeare's *Merry Wives of Windsor*, used a ferry and from 1706 a wooden bridge. This was replaced in 1811 by a half wooden (on the left Buckinghamshire side) and half iron (on the Berkshire bank) bridge which lasted until the Victoria and Albert Bridges succeeded the Datchet crossing. The much restored Datchet church has a 13th-century chancel with memorials to Lady Katheryn Barkeley, wife of Elizabeth I's Standard Bearer, and Christopher Barker who was the Queen's printer. A milestone opposite records London 20 miles and Windsor 1 mile. The upstream riverside path opened in 1995 on Sumptermead Ait (still an island thanks to a narrow channel) which affords a good view of the Royal Boathouse where the Royal Barge (now at the National Maritime Museum) was kept until 1953.

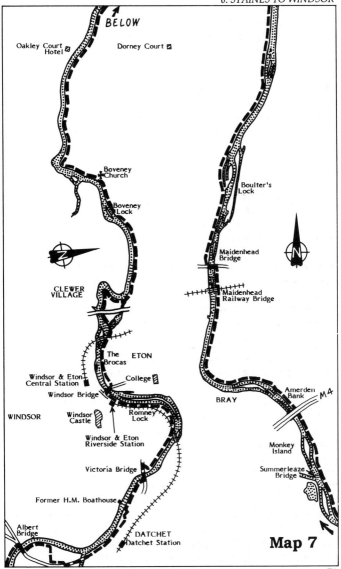

BELOW

Oakley Court Hotel

Dorney Court

Boveney Church

Boveney Lock

Boulter's Lock

Maidenhead Bridge

Maidenhead Railway Bridge

CLEWER VILLAGE

The Brocas

ETON

Windsor & Eton Central Station

College

Windsor Bridge

WINDSOR

Windsor Castle

Romney Lock

BRAY

Amerden Bank

M4

Windsor & Eton Riverside Station

Victoria Bridge

Monkey Island

Summerleaze Bridge

Former H.M. Boathouse

Albert Bridge

DATCHET

Datchet Station

Map 7

Continue along the road on the pavement and when the houses end turn left through a gate. A path runs down a slope to cross a backwater on to Sumptermead Ait. The way is along the stream for a short distance before bearing left to the riverside opposite the Royal Boathouse. Follow the winding path which crosses a small footbridge and later a more substantial bridge over the sometimes dry upstream end of the narrow channel. Go ahead over the grass and up steep steps to a gate on Victoria Bridge.

VICTORIA BRIDGE gives the first good view of Windsor Castle - as seen by the Queen's guests, such as King Juan Carlos and Polish President Lech Walesa, who have arrived here on state visits to be welcomed in this northern part of The Home Park before joining a carriage procession to the Castle.

Cross Victoria Bridge and at the end of the white railing (right) turn right back to the riverside where the towpath can be joined again. The path runs along the edge of the public section of Home Park and under Black Pott's railway bridge.

BLACK POTT'S BRIDGE, erected in 1849 to carry the Waterloo-Windsor railway line, was designed by Sir Joseph Lock and decorated by Sir William Tite who was making the nearby station look regal. The crossing was slightly altered in 1892. The origin of the name is uncertain but this spot has been known as Black Pott's for at least 300 years when a fishing lodge on the far bank was used by Charles II and Izaac Walton.

The riverbank, rich in wildflowers, has a view of Eton's playing fields beyond an island. During May's Royal Windsor Horse Show the path has stables to the left. At a kissing gate go through a boatyard to a lane which avoids Romney Lock. Soon there is a view of Eton College Chapel. Turn right into the fenced Romney Walk which is by the river and leads to The Donkey House. Continue ahead to Windsor Bridge.

Busy river upstream of Windsor's Victoria Bridge

Refreshments

Bell Weir Lock: Runnymede Hotel.

Runnymede: Runnymede Tearoom (run by National Trust in lodge). Apr-Sep 10.30am-5.30pm.

Datchet: The Bridge (next to The Stag). Coffee and teas. 9am-3.30pm (not Sun).

Accommodation

Staines: The Swan (right bank by bridge) (01784 452494).

Staines: Albany House, 2 Glebe Road, TW18 1BX (01784 441223).

Bell Weir Lock: Runnymede Hotel, Windsor Rd, Egham (01784 436171).

Datchet: 55 London Road, SL3 9JY (01753 580401).

Transport

Staines: Rail (South West Trains).

Datchet: Rail (South West Trains).

Windsor: Rail from Windsor & Eton Riverside (South West Trains) or Windsor & Eton Central (Thames Trains).

Map

OS Landranger 176 (West London).

Boveney Church

7. Windsor to Maidenhead
6½ miles

The rural towpath remains on the Buckinghamshire bank with views of a film set house and Bray village before passing under Maidenhead's Brunel bridge. There are no refreshments on the towpath between Windsor and Maidenhead except in season at Bray Lock.

WINDSOR is derived from the Anglo-Saxon 'Wyndesore' meaning 'winding shore' which probably refers to the Thames' twisting course. The castle, begun as a fortress by William the Conqueror, is the Queen's main home and the resting place of many past monarchs including Henry VI. The exterior is the result of extensive restoration by Sir Jeffry Wyatville for George IV. When a massive fire swept the west end in 1992 water was pumped from the Thames and two years later stone for the restoration came by barge. The only painting destroyed was one which George III had wanted to burn almost 200 years earlier. He also gave Franz de Cleyn's painting *The Last Supper* to the parish church where curate J.S. Stone wrote the hymn *The Church's One Foundation*. The nextdoor Guildhall was designed by Sir Christopher Wren who had to add extra pillars (in fact not quite touching the ceiling) because the council thought it looked unsafe. Almost opposite is a plaque recalling H.G. Wells' apprenticeship to a draper portrayed in *Kipps* and *The History of Mr Polly*.

WINDSOR BRIDGE is at least an 800 year old crossing point. Both road and river traffic paid tolls and in 1736 it was possible to walk over alive for 2d whilst being carried in a coffin cost 6s. 8d. Tolls ended in 1897 after court proceedings but the toll-keeper's cottage remains as part of The Old House Hotel on the Windsor bank. The present 1822 bridge was the first arched bridge on the river. Road traffic was banned in 1970. Until Eton College's 550th anniversary in 1990 boys were not allowed over the bridge into Windsor unless wearing a tie and jacket.

Although the towpath continues briefly on the Windsor bank to a ferry (summer only) the Thames Path crosses the bridge to Eton.

ETON College, dominating the village, was inspired by Winchester College and founded by Henry VI. Seventy poor scholars formed the school nucleus and today there are are still 70 'King's Scholars' although most of the school consists of 'Oppidans' paying fees. The chapel was built in the 15th century with the intention of adding a nave to what is really just the east end choir. Part of the uniform is a black tail coat worn in mourning for George III. Eton's upstream riverside is known as The Brocas after the Brocas family who gave the land to the College - Sir John de Brocas from Gascony was one of the Black Prince's favourite knights.

Turn left down Brocas Street. Beyond the Waterman's Arms and the Eton College boathouse there is The Brocas meadow where the towpath joins at the ferry point and main mooring. The way is over grass with a fine view back to the Castle. After the wood there is a railway bridge.

Windsor Castle from The Brocas

WINDSOR GREAT WESTERN BRIDGE, carrying the Great Western Railway (GWR) branch line from Slough, was designed by Brunel and opened in 1849 just months ahead of the London & South Western Railway which was building the Black Pott's Bridge.

After two footbridges (the first is Lower Bargeman's Bridge) over Cuckoo Weir, the path is on an island only spoilt by the Queen Elizabeth (Windsor relief road) Bridge. On the far bank beyond the by-pass is Clewer Church on the Mill Stream.

CLEWER William the Conqueror attended services at St Andrew's. Buried in the south-west corner of the churchyard (noted for its wild flowers) is Sir Daniel Gooch, GWR's first locomotive engineer who decided to make Swindon a railway centre. Also buried there is Nanny May (Mary Ann Hull) who looked after Queen Victoria's children as listed on the stone. The church gatehouse is a local history museum. The convent in nearby Hatch Lane once received prostitutes sent by William Gladstone from London for rehabilitation.

(Clewer church and YHA hostel can be reached by going up the path on the upstream side of the by-pass bridge, over the bridge and down into the village. Follow the road round to the right to pass the church. Turn left at the end of the road for the YHA.)

Although the main path now cuts the corner, the Thames Path stays with the towpath. The paths are united at a bridge when the towpath leaves the island. There is a view of Eton Wick inland. Behind the trees on the far bank is Windsor Race Course and by the path there is soon a riverside seat at a spot known as Athens.

ATHENS was an Eton College bathing spot where rules required that "boys who are undressed must either get at once into the water or get behind screens when boats containing ladies come in sight".

Soon after Boveney Lock there is a last view of Windsor Castle - the upper turret and flagpole can just be seen above the trees. Soon there is Boveney Church.

BOVENEY CHURCH, which has a Norman window, may have been a chapel for nearby Bolney Court which belonged to Burnham

Abbey 3 miles north. Regular services are no longer held and the church is usually locked but information for obtaining the key is on the board. Windsor Forest timber is thought to have been landed here.

After lonely Andrew's Boat House the river bends to give a view of substantial riverside houses at Ruddle's Pool and then Windsor Marina. After a mile the path is level with Oakley Court which will have been glimpsed ahead.

OAKLEY COURT was built in 1859 as a residence for an Englishman who hoped the gothic style would make his homesick French wife happy. General de Gaulle is the most famous Frenchman to have visited. In 1950 the house was purchased by Hammer Films who used it for making *St Trinian's, Half a Sixpence* and *The Rocky Horror Picture Show*. In 1970 the 92 bedroom mansion became a hotel.

Just beyond Queen's Eyot is Bray Marina on the far bank. Here on the towpath an unmarked footpath leads inland passing through Wallbank Grove (planted 1996) to Dorney Court.

DORNEY COURT dates from about 1440 and stands on slight high ground to avoid flooding. The house, "one of the finest Tudor manor houses", has been the home of the Palmer family since 1600 and among the portraits is Sir James Palmer, Governor of the Mortlake Tapestry Works. Dorney means 'bee island' and honey is sold here where England's first pineapple may have been grown and given to Charles II who visited here. The church dates from the Norman period. The house, used as 'Syon' in the film *Lady Jane*, is open on Bank Holidays in May (and the preceding Sun) and Mon-Thu Jul-Aug; 1-4.30pm; admission charge.

A short distance beyond the Dorney footpath turning, the towpath passes under Summerleaze Bridge.

SUMMERLEAZE BRIDGE opened in 1996 as both a footbridge for public use and a support for a conveyor belt carrying gravel from an excavation for a rowing lake on the towpath side to the Bray bank. When completed the $1^{1}/_{2}$ mile course developed by Eton College will be known as the Dorney Lake Park and Nature Reserve.

Just before reaching a line of residences, where the path is

well maintained, there is the beginning of Monkey Island.

MONKEY ISLAND probably means 'monks island' as it belonged to Merton Priory on the River Wandle which had a house upstream at Amerden Bank. But in 1738 the 3rd Duke of Marlborough decorated the fishing lodge ceiling with monkeys. The island's foundations for building had been strengthened when barges brought rubble from London after the 1666 Great Fire. The lodge has been a hotel since 1840. Edward VII and Queen Alexandra had tea on the lawn with three future sovereigns - George V, Edward VIII and George VI. H.G. Wells visited several times with Rebecca West who describes the island in her novel *Return of the Soldier*. The island could only be reached by boat until a footbridge was built from the right bank in 1956. The 'Birmingham Six' spent their first night of freedom here in secret after being released from prison in 1991.

Beyond a gate the way is through a copse and under the M4 Bridge (1961) to Amerden Bank. Soon there is Bray Lock and, after Headpile Eyot, a clear view of Bray village on the Berkshire bank. A seat is directly opposite The Waterside Inn.

BRAY is famous for the song *Vicar of Bray* although which one is uncertain. Simon Alwyn adapted to the many changes of the Reformation years but the song probably refers to the Stuart times. The church is early 14th-century and among those married there is snooker player Steve Davies. The village is noted for celebrities including Rolf Harris who came because it reminded him of his "river's edge home in Perth". Gerald Ratner lived at upstream Somerville (with the American wrap-around balcony). On the Waterside Inn jetty is the warning 'restaurant only' in case anyone thinks it's still The George pub rather than Michael Roux's 3 star establishment opened in 1972. Diners have included the Duke and Duchess of York who came just two days after announcing their separation. Journalist John MacCarthy met friend and campaigner Jill Morrell whilst on an outing to the inn - the group made alternative arrangements when they saw the expensive menu. The inn is next to Ferry Lane but a ferry no longer runs across to the seat.

On reaching a house the path is gravelled and then metalled to pass under Maidenhead Railway Bridge.

MAIDENHEAD RAILWAY BRIDGE, completed by Brunel in 1839, carries the Paddington-Bristol railway line and appears in J.M.W. Turner's 1844 painting *Rain, Steam and Speed on the GWR*. These are the largest and flattest brick arches ever built and many thought they would collapse under the first train. A shout or whistle from below will echo. The bridge, widened in 1893, partly rests on Guards Club Island - the club was on the far bank.

Continue ahead along the road to go left at the end of a white boathouse (due for redevelopment) back to the waterside. The path runs in front of a derelict building and under Maidenhead Bridge to a gate. Bear round to the right through a small boatyard to another gate at the side of Skindles. Go right to the main road and right again over the bridge to pass from Taplow to Maidenhead.

Refreshments

Bray Lock: Ice cream and drinks available in summer.

Accommodation

Windsor: The Laurells, 22 Dedworth Rd, SL4 5AH (01753 855821).

Windsor: 57 Grove Rd, SL4 1JD (01753 853600).

Windsor: Dee & Steve's B&B, 169 Oxford Road, SL4 5DX (01753 854489).

Clewer: YHA, Edgeworth House, Mill Lane, Clewer, Windsor SL4 5JE (01753 861710).

Amerden Bank: Caravan & Camping site (01628 627461). Apr-Oct. Between M4 Bridge and Bray Lock.

Transport

Windsor: Rail to Windsor & Eton Riverside (South West Trains) or Windsor & Eton Central (Thames Trains).

Maidenhead: Rail (Thames Trains).

Tourist Information

Windsor: 24 High Street, SL4 1LH (01753 743900).

Map

OS Landranger 175 (Reading & Windsor).

8. Maidenhead to Marlow

7 miles

This is one of the very attractive stretches of the river and rich in heritage. After the most famous lock there is Cliveden Reach and a rare diversion from the riverbank to pass through Cookham, made famous by artist Stanley Spencer. The way is then along the edge of rare marshland before turning a corner into the attractive Chiltern town of Marlow.

MAIDENHEAD BRIDGE There has been a bridge here on the main London road, linking Maidenhead (right bank) with Taplow, since the mid 13th century when a hermit collected tolls. It was over a much repaired wooden bridge that William of Orange passed in 1688 to accept the Crown in London. The present bridge, completed in 1777, is similar to Swinford Bridge, also designed by Sir Robert Taylor. The latter retains its tolls but charges ceased here in 1903 after an enquiry exposed misuse of revenues. Skindles on the left upstream bank was The Orkney Arms until 1833 when William Skindle turned it from a coaching inn into a fashionable hotel.

On the Maidenhead side go upstream through a public garden to join Ray Mead Road. Beyond a riverside building go right to reach Chandler's Quay where the path crosses Clapper's Stream. Rejoin the road and soon after Riverside Gardens there is Boulter's Lock.

BOULTER'S LOCK, the river's longest and deepest, was once the busiest. It is still the most famous thanks to E.J. Gregory's 1898 painting *Boulter's Lock - Sunday Afternoon* showing the lock packed with small pleasure craft when ex-Naval cutlass instructor W.H. Turner was lock-keeper. The mill stream runs between Boulter's Island and Ray Mill Island which is reached by a bridge. The Boulter's Lock Hotel was built in 1726 for the miller - the first in 1348 was called Ray and in 1773 Richard Ray became lock-keeper. 'Boulter', derived from 'bolter' meaning 'miller', gave its name to the lock from 1847.

After 100 yards the road leaves the river and the path continues beyond a TC gate.

TC GATE This is the first of the grey-blue Thames Conservancy gates on the towpath. Each is numbered with the lowest being at Lechlade although number 1 has gone. New gates erected by the successor NRA (now Environment Agency) are dark wood.

Soon on the left there is the restored former Maidenhead Court Boathouse. The most impressive of the substantial Victorian residences is the last - Islet Park House - where White Brook serves as an approach to its boathouse. After the path has run inside a line of trees there is the first view of Cliveden on high ground above the woods. Inland there are fields and after ½ mile the path is level with the first building, Spring Cottage, in Cliveden's grounds.

CLIVEDEN The first house on the prime plateau site above the river was begun in 1666 for the 2nd Duke of Buckingham. The present building is by Charles Barry of Parliament fame. William Waldorf Astor became known as 'walled off Astor' when he moved in declaring America to be no fit place for a gentleman. His daughter-in-law Nancy became the first woman MP and Cliveden's hostess, entertaining such people as Henry James, Hilaire Belloc, Charlie Chaplin, Bernard Shaw, Lawrence of Arabia and Oswald Mosley. Winston Churchill's comment on her crowded parties was: "Thirty dishes and no damn room to eat them!" Later Cliveden was called "Britain's most notorious country house" after Spring Cottage featured in the Profumo affair. When told the mansion was to become a hotel Harold Macmillan commented: "My dear boy, it always has been." In 1989 actors Kenneth Branagh and Emma Thompson were married in the grounds which are open to the public.

The towpath switches bank at the former My Lady Ferry.

MY LADY FERRY, the last operated by Thames Conservancy, ran until 1956. The towing horses had to be moved to the left bank for just under ½ mile before returning to the right bank to go up Cookham Lock Cut on its left side. The operation between here and Cookham Bridge involved three ferries. Ferry Cottage opposite is

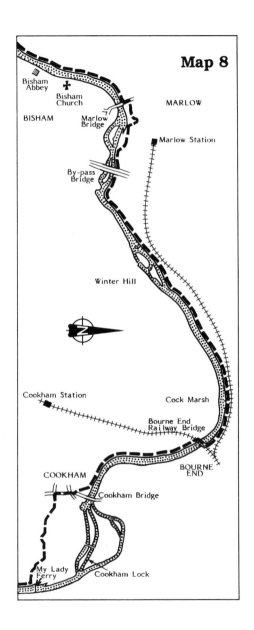

Map 8

Bisham Abbey

Bisham Church

MARLOW

BISHAM

Marlow Bridge

Marlow Station

By-pass Bridge

Winter Hill

Cookham Station

Cock Marsh

Bourne End Railway Bridge

BOURNE END

COOKHAM

Cookham Bridge

My Lady Ferry

Cookham Lock

rented out as a holiday cottage by the National Trust with the short stretch of towpath outside still a public footpath.

The Thames Path now turns inland through a wood and parallel with a drive. Beyond a stile bear half left towards the white house with a high hedge. The enclosed path runs round to join Mill Lane. Turn left to walk into Cookham. At a junction go right for the village centre.

COOKHAM The church, scene of many weddings including actress Susan George's in 1984, has a 12th-century nave. The churchyard features in Stanley Spencer's painting *The Resurrection* - the artist's grave is to left of the path at a point where the view and painting can be compared. He was born at Fernlea in the High Street near the Methodist Church which is now the Stanley Spencer Gallery - England's only gallery devoted to a 20th-century artist (1891-1959). *Christ Preaching at Cookham Regatta* is set at the back of The Ferry Inn and in *The Crucifixion* the tormentors are said to be based on local faces. He said: "You can't walk by the river at Cliveden Reach and not believe in God." Cookham Bridge, which appears in his *Swan Upping*, was built in 1867 to replace the original of 1840. The tollhouse, which operated until 1947, is on the far bank. Lullebrook Manor in Ferry Lane is said to be the inspiration for 'Toad Hall' in *The Wind in the Willows* - its author Kenneth Grahame lived nearby when the manor's owner was the first person in the village to have a motor car.

Continue past the High Street (left) and Odney Lane (right) to go left by timber-framed cottages into the churchyard. Take the main path to the left of the church to find the river beyond a narrow kissing gate. The walk continues to the left upstream, past the sailing club and along the edge of Cock Marsh opposite the mainly Edwardian houses of Bourne End.

COCK MARSH is one of the few remaining examples of lowland marsh and an exceptionally good site for seeing redshank, lapwing and wading birds. The burial mounds west of the railway are evidence of Bronze Age occupation.

Beyond the kissing gate into the National Trust area keep to the right of the belt of trees. On the far bank the River Wye (which

rises at West Wycombe) can be seen joining the Thames near Andrew's Boathouses. Go through the gate to pass under the railway bridge.

BOURNE END RAILWAY BRIDGE succeeded an 1857 wooden structure carrying a single track. The present iron and steel bridge was opened in 1894 with provision for a second track. The line no longer runs to High Wycombe but carries just the single track for the Maidenhead-Marlow shuttle. The footbridge was attached in 1993 for the Thames Path to save a long walk over Winter Hill. Before this there was an electric bell on a Bourne End bank tree for those wanting to be rowed over to The Bounty pub on the Cock Marsh side. Author Enid Blyton lived at the Old Thatch in Bourne End from 1929 to 1937.

Ahead is The Bounty but the Thames Path leaves the towpath to continue over the bridge. Once on the Bourne End side turn upstream on a footpath running near the river and through a boatyard. The path soon passes through the Upper Thames Sailing Club grounds before running behind riverside gardens to Spade Oak Farm by a level crossing. Go through the kissing gate ahead to an old ferry point.

SPADE OAK FERRY, which ceased running in 1962, is where the towpath crosses the river. Ferry Cottage can be seen opposite with Winter Hill at the back of Cock Marsh.

The way ahead is through a series of towpath gates and past two islands. Later there is a view of an impressive castellated house. The path has a gravel surface as the river turns west below Quarry Wood to pass Longridge Scout Boating Centre on the far bank and go under Marlow By-pass.

MARLOW BY-PASS, completed in 1972, was the walkers' crossing before the Bourne End footbridge opened. Quarry Wood opposite may be the 'wild wood' in *The Wind in the Willows*.

Beyond a line of houses there is a field. Only navigation can reach the lock so the towpath bears inland to a road. Turn left at Mill Road to follow an S bend past Marlow Mill (left) and The Mill House (right).

MARLOW MILL The mill in the early 19th century embraced three mills including one producing England's first brass thimbles which were taken upstream to a warehouse on the City of London's Brocken Wharf. Mill House was home of author Sir Evelyn Wrench who founded the English Speaking Union and Royal Overseas League.

There is a view of Marlow's weir, suspension bridge and church before the road turns inland. Follow the wall and go left along Seven Corner Alley which leads to St Peter Street and The Two Brewers.

THE TWO BREWERS was frequented by Jerome K. Jerome who is said to have worked on part of *Three Men in a Boat* here although most was written in a Chelsea flat. The Queen's Swan Master and other Swan Uppers visit the pub every summer during their progress upstream checking on swans. Until recently the sign showed Thomas Wethered, founder of Marlow's brewery, on one side and Samuel Whitbread, who bought Wethered's, on the other. Seven Corner Alley, alongside the pub, was used by towing horses being led between the lock and Marlow Bridge which until 1832 was at the end of St Peter Street. Until 1773 there was also a winch at the end of the road for hauling barges over a flash lock on the site of the weir.

Cross St Peter Street to go down a second alley by The Old Malt House opposite The Two Brewers to reach the Marlow's churchyard and The Causeway.

Refreshments

Maidenhead: Riverside Gardens tea hut open most days.

Cookham: Church Hall. Teas 3.15-5.15pm May-Sep weekends.

Cookham: The Two Roses, High Street. Lunches, teas & dinners.

Cookham: The Ferry Inn (Harvester) by bridge. Open all day.

Cock Marsh: The Bounty pub. Open usual day & evening hours in summer. In winter open Sun lunchtime only.

Accommodation

Maidenhead: Sheephouse Manor, Sheephouse Road, SL6 8HJ (01628 776902).

Maidenhead: Ray Corner Guest House, 141 Bridge Road, SL6 8NQ (01628 32784).

Maidenhead: Gables End, 4 Gables Close, SL6 8QD (01628 39630).

Maidenhead Bridge (Taplow side): Bridge Cottage Guest House, Bath Road, SL6 0AR (01628 26805).

Cookham: Wylie Cottage, School Lane, SL6 9QJ (01628 520106).

Transport

Maidenhead: Rail (Thames Trains).

Cookham: Rail (Thames Trains).

Marlow: Rail (Thames Trains

Tourist Information

Maidenhead: Library, St Ives Road, SL6 1QU (01628 781110).

Map

OS Landranger 175 (Reading & Windsor).

Temple Bridge near Bisham

9. Marlow to Henley

8¹/₂ miles

Only thanks to a new bridge is it possible to again follow the river all the way from Marlow to Henley. On this stretch the path passes through three counties and alongside three ancient monastic sites before reaching the straight rowing course leading to Henley Bridge.

MARLOW The 1835 All Saints replaced the 12th-century church undermined by centuries of flooding. In the porch is a memorial (oldest erected at public expense) to Sir Miles Hobart who started the House of Commons custom of slamming the door in Black Rod's face - his death caused by bolting horses on Holborn Hill is depicted. Artist E.J. Gregory, who lived at 100 High Street, is buried in the churchyard. Next to the partly 14th-century Old Parsonage in St Peter's Street is St Peter's (RC), by Pugin, which has St James the Great's hand (not displayed). Poet Percy Shelley, who kept a skiff

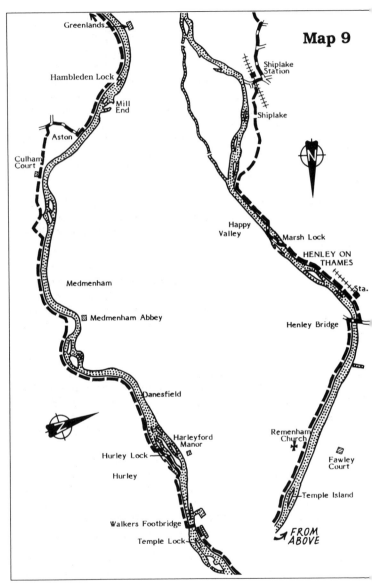

Map 9

Greenlands

Hambleden Lock

Mill End

Aston

Culham Court

Shiplake Station

Shiplake

N

Happy Valley

Marsh Lock

HENLEY ON THAMES

Sta.

Medmenham

Medmenham Abbey

Henley Bridge

Danesfield

Harleyford Manor

Hurley Lock

Hurley

Remenham Church

Fawley Court

Temple Island

Walkers Footbridge

Temple Lock

FROM ABOVE

for Thames expeditions, lived at Albion House (marked by plaque) in West Street in 1817 writing *The Revolt of Islam* whilst his wife Mary produced *Frankenstein*. Earlier they had lived with Thomas Love Peacock at number 67 (now a car park). A century on T.S. Eliot lived at number 31 (an old Post Office). The present bridge, based on Hammersmith Bridge, opened in 1832. The mansion in Higginson Park just upstream of the bridge was built in the 1760s for mental illness specialist Dr William Battie - hence the term 'batty'. The Compleat Angler hotel on the Berkshire bank stands on the spot where Izaak Walton is supposed to have written *The Compleat Angler* in 1653.

Walk to the bridge and keep right to follow a path down the side to the towpath. Beyond the town mooring at Higginson Park there is a view over the water to Bisham Church and the nextdoor Abbey.

BISHAM CHURCH, with its landmark Norman tower, has been called "a jewel on the riverside". Floodwater can reach the pulpit. Buried in a magnificent chapel is diplomat Sir Philip Hoby whose body was brought by river from his Blackfriars house in 1588. It was on this reach that Shelley spent much time floating in a skiff writing *The Revolt of Islam* which features a river and a boat.

BISHAM ABBEY belongs to the Sports Council. The first building was occupied by the Knights Templars in 1139 but after their suppression in 1307 an Augustinian Priory was established. Warwick the King-maker was buried here in 1471 after the Battle of Barnet. Although closed by Henry VIII in 1536, the monastery soon re-opened as an abbey for Benedictines displaced from Chertsey who were to pray for the late Queen Jane (Seymour). But in the following year it too was dissolved by the King who later gave the property to his second Queen, Anne of Cleves, as a consolation for her divorce. She did a swop with Philip Hoby for his house in Kent. The future Elizabeth I spent three years here and returned as Queen in 1597. The Abbey is the England Football Team Headquarters.

Soon the towpath comes level with Temple Mill Island.

TEMPLE MILL ISLAND takes its name from the Templars who ran the mill. In 1710 this was a copper foundry which was enlarged when the opening of the Thames & Severn Canal made it possible to bring copper by water from Swansea. In 1722 Daniel Defoe, who had just written *Robinson Crusoe*, called and found brass kettles and pans being made. In 1848 production switched to brown paper and continued until 1969. The building, which had the largest mill wheel on the river, made way for the marina development at the end of the 1970s.

Beyond Temple Lock the towpath crosses Temple Bridge to the Berkshire bank.

TEMPLE BRIDGE, a 150ft span, is Britain's longest hardwood footbridge which in 1989 replaced a ferry which had not operated since 1953.

Continue upstream under a line of trees with a view half right of Harleyford Manor.

HARLEYFORD MANOR, another house (now offices) said to be the inspiration for Kenneth Grahame's 'Toad Hall', was built in 1755 by architect Sir Robert Taylor for Sir Robert Clayton.

The towpath crosses a high bridge on to Hurley's lock island. On returning to the mainland after Hurley Lock keep ahead down steps only to visit Hurley village.

HURLEY is hidden from the towpath. The church was the chapel of a Benedictine priory consecrated in 1086 by St Osmund. Edward the Confessor's wife is buried in an unmarked grave. The refectory is now a private house but the guest house continues in business as Ye Olde Bell. Lady Place stands on the site of a building where James II's overthrow was planned by Protestants. Later a grateful William of Orange paid a visit. Elizabeth II embarked here for Runnymede in 1964. Wooden boats are built here by Peter Freebody whose family has worked on the river since at least the 13th century. His ancestor John was working as a bargeman on the same riverside site in 1642.

The towpath continues upstream, over the high bridge at a boatyard inlet and through a small gate into a large meadow. The far bank is a high cliff. The river bends south and after a kissing

gate it is possible to look back and see Danesfield on top of the cliff.

DANESFIELD takes it name from the Danes who came upstream and built a strategic fortification. The mansion, faced with local stone and designed by Romaine Walker, was completed in 1901 for Robert Hudson of Hudson's Soap fame. After being an RAF station (1941-77) it opened as a hotel in 1991. The previous house on the site was home of Charles Scott-Murray who added a chapel (demolished) by Pugin housing the St James' hand.

The path joins a road in front of riverside homes at Frogmill. At Xamaron (left) bear half right to stay by the water as the main path veers away by a former barn. (For The Black Boy Inn turn left at the end of the houses.) The towpath runs past three islands. Beyond here the Thames Path keeps ahead through a gate to cut a corner and run directly to Medmenham Ferry. But for a good view of Medmenham Abbey stay on the towpath.

MEDMENHAM ABBEY was a Cistercian foundation begun in 1201 and closed in 1536 when the community comprised of only the Abbot and one monk. There is a remaining 13th-century pillar but the attractive ruins are largely contrived. The building is best known for Sir Francis Dashwood's notorious Hell Fire Club which met there between 1750 and 1774. Members, who included John Wilkes and Lord Sandwich, were known as 'Franciscans of Medmenham' after their host was alleged to have performed obscene parodies of religious rites. The ferry was used by Charles II, Edward VII and George V who was accompanied by Queen Mary. Although an historic 1899 court ruling confirmed the public's right to use this navigation ferry it has ceased operation.

At the ferry point the towpath switches banks leaving the Thames Path to continue on the right bank through a kissing gate. There are three ditches crossed by footbridges. Beyond the third one bear half left across a field to find a kissing gate in the middle of the far side. Turn right along a track which runs uphill past a pink cottage. Go through a kissing gate where the track divides near a nursery. Keep ahead over a field to pass through four kissing gates flanking the vista between Culham Court and the

Thames below.

CULHAM COURT was built in 1770 but its architect is unknown. When Lord De La Warr's brother entertained George III fresh breakfast rolls wrapped in warm flannels were rushed down from London by horse relay. The house was home of Lady Barber, who founded Birmingham's Barber Institute of Fine Arts in 1932, and from 1948 it was owned by banker and arts patron Michael Behrens. In the garden can be seen modern sculpture including a duplicate of Elizabeth Frink's *Striding Madonna* which stands outside Salisbury Cathedral. Architect Raymond Erith redesigned the garden on both sides of the house.

Keep along the top of a ridge to pass a cluster of trees (left) and reach a kissing gate at the far end of the field. Keep forward to follow the road ahead downhill to Aston. Turn right to reach The Flower Pot.

THE FLOWER POT advertised "Boatman always in attendance" in 1893 but the ferry bringing the towpath back to this side has ceased to run. However, still painted on the inn's outside wall is "good accommodation for fishing and boating parties". Henley beer and substantial sandwiches are available and there are old Thames prints on the wall. Chickens run around the garden.

Continue past the inn (left) down Ferry Lane to join the towpath which returns to this bank at the end of the road. Soon there is a view of Hambleden Mill and Lock.

HAMBLEDEN MILL was working until 1955 having been in existence since the 13th century. A 300 yard narrow public footpath runs across the weir from the lock to the mill.

The Thames Path stays on the right bank beyond the lock. After a short distance the grass gives way to a hard surface which continues all the way to Henley. Soon there is a view of a white mansion, Greenlands, on the far bank below the beechwoods on the Chiltern hillsides.

GREENLANDS, built in 1853, was the home of bookseller W.H. Smith. When First Lord of the Admiralty he was lampooned in

Gilbert and Sullivan's *HMS Pinafore* as "Ruler of the Queen's Navee". Since 1946 the house has been occupied by Henley Management College. In the Civil War the original 1604 building was bombarded from across the water by Cromwellian forces flushing out Royalists.

The towpath turns south to approach the Henley Regatta course which runs from Temple Island to Henley Bridge.

TEMPLE ISLAND, sometimes called Regatta Island and now owned by Henley Royal Regatta, once belonged to Fawley Court just upstream on the far bank. The 'temple', intended as a focus for a vista from the mansion, is a fishing lodge designed in 1771 by James Wyatt who added frescoes inside.

After 400 yards the towpath reaches Remenham which faces Fawley Court.

REMENHAM is a hamlet with a church serving a huge parish. St Nicholas' tower dates from 1836 and the main building restored in 1870 has an apse built on the line of the Norman predecessor. Actress Jenny Agutter was married here. Buried in the churchyard is Caled Gould who died in 1836 aged 92 having been Hambleden lock-keeper since 1777. Descendant Bryan Gould had a London Thames-side home when he was an MP.

FAWLEY COURT on the left bank has been known as 'Poland-on-Thames' since 1953 when the house became a school for the sons of exiled Poles. The rebuilding in the 1680s followed the sacking of the house by Royalists in the Civil War. Visitors have included William III and William IV.

The first white riverside house on the towpath beyond Remenham is Barn Elms.

BARN ELMS was home of actress Gladys Cooper from the early Fifties until her death here in 1971. She walked the towpath daily even in her last year. The gleaming white building has since 1990 been home of rowing veteran Dr Walter Scott who spotted the house whilst competing in the Royal Regatta.

Just before the bridge there is the Leander Club.

LEANDER CLUB, founded in 1818, is Britain's oldest rowing club. Members include Olympic medallists. The building was erected in 1897 - exactly a century before women were admitted as members.

Cross Henley Bridge to leave Berkshire and enter Henley on the Oxfordshire bank.

Refreshments

Marlow: Burger's, corner of The Causeway and Station Road. Celebrated baker's taken over by Swiss Berger family in 1942 and now producing 32 kinds of chocolate. Tearoom open daily except Sun serving tea and high tea until 6pm.

Marlow: Church Hall near Burger's. Teas May-Sep Sun & Bank Hols 3-6pm.

Hurley: The Rising Sun.

Hurley: Teas at Church. Jun-Sep Sun 2-5pm.

Frogmill: The Black Boy Inn. 16th-century and 500 yards inland on Henley Road. 11.30am-2.30pm & 6-11pm. (Sun 12-2.30pm & 7-10.30pm).

Aston: The Flower Pot. 10.30am-3pm & 6-11pm; Sun 12-3pm & 7-10.30pm. Breakfast 8-10am in summer.

Accommodation

Marlow: 5 Pound Lane, SL7 2AE (01628 482649).

Marlow: 10 Lock Road, SL7 1QP (01628 473875).

Marlow: Huxley, 18 Lock Road, SL7 1QW (01628 487741).

Hurley: Lock Island camping site (01628 824334). Apr-Sep.

Hurley: Caravan & Camping Park (01628) 823501). Mar-Oct. Upstream from lock at back of meadow.

Frogmill: The Black Boy Inn. See above (01628 824212).

Aston: The Flower Pot. See above (01491 574721).

Transport

Marlow: Rail (Thames Trains).

Henley: Rail (Thames Trains).

Tourist Information

Marlow: 31 High Street, SL7 1AU (01628 483597).

Map

OS Landranger 175 (Reading & Windsor).

Henley-on-Thames
Mapledurham House

10. Henley to Reading

9 miles

The exit from Henley is as attractive as the entry from the north. At Marsh Lock the towpath runs out on a long wooden walkway into the middle of the river before passing Happy Valley. After Shiplake, where the water is briefly lost behind riverside residences, the Thames is a green corridor into Reading by way of attractive Sonning.

HENLEY-ON-THAMES Church, first recorded in 1204, was served by Dorchester monks. The present building dates from about 1400 like nextdoor Chantry House. The church tower, built about 1550, contains a monument to William Hayward who, just before his death in 1782, designed Henley Bridge described by Horace Walpole as "the most beautiful in the world after the Ponti di Triniti at Florence". Henley's earlier 14th-century bridge had buildings including a chapel. Outside the church's north-west door is the tomb of Richard Jennings who headed the St Paul's Cathedral building team. The Sacred Heart Church, in Vicarage Road towards the south of the town, incorporates the east end of Danesfield's chapel. The Angel is 18th-century and now looks across the water not at The Carpenters Arms but Terry Farrell's Henley Royal Regatta HQ. The Regatta, founded in 1839, is held during the first week in July. The first University Boat Race was rowed here in 1929. Charles I stayed twice at The Red Lion and in Hart Street is Speaker's House, birthplace of Speaker Lenthall who was confronted in the chamber by the King. In John Mortimer's *Paradise Postponed* this is 'Hartscombe' town. Brakspeare's brewery (a corporate member of the locally based Open Spaces Society) sometimes provides a distinctive aroma along the waterfront. The River & Rowing Museum building, designed by David Chipperfield and inspired by Oxfordshire barns, opened in 1998 on Mill Marsh

---

Dorchester's bathing spot next Thames confluence with the Thame

Meadows (see below). The museum (01491 415600) is open daily.

From the bridge turn upstream behind The Angel. At Hobbs & Sons the traffic leaves the towpath which soon runs past Mill Marsh Meadows park which has the River & Rowing Museum behind the trees. Just beyond The Old House turn left on to a long wooden bridge running out to Marsh Lock.

MARSH LOCK The reason for the long wooden walkway across the weirstream to the lock and back is that there was a mill, used for a brass foundry, in the way. A flour mill was on the right bank which is still known as Mill Bank.

Soon after returning to the left bank there is a gate on the Henley boundary (a marker to the right). The way is now along-side a meadow with a view soon across the water to a rustic bridge over the end of Happy Valley.

HAPPY VALLEY The bridge carrying the Henley-Wargrave road was built in 1900 with stone from Reading Abbey. The valley beyond is in the grounds of Park Place, seat of the Duke of Hamilton in the 18th century.

Along this reach are 1908 Conservancy markers to indicate a once 14ft wide towpath - which shows how much erosion has occurred. The river bends at the former Bolney Ferry, just down-stream of Ferry Ayot, where the towpath crosses the river. Con-tinue on the Thames Path as it heads half right inland to a footbridge and stile. The way is enclosed as it passes Bolney Ferry Boat House to run between a polo ground (right) and Thames-Side Court's garden and railway.

THAMES-SIDE COURT, built in 1914, is the home of Urs Schwarzenback who in the early 1990s landscaped the 8 acre garden and added the extensive narrow gauge railway running alongside the river.

On meeting Bolney Road continue ahead keeping left at a fork.

BOLNEY ROAD Most of the riverside houses are Edwardian and one has a narrow gauge railway (narrower than Thames-Side;

Towpath at Marsh Lock

above). Past riverside residents here have included playwright Terence Rattigan and fashion designer Norman Hartnell.

Just before a house called Eyot Wood (left) and a new (1996) house go half right up a narrow footpath leading to the railway line. Do not cross the line but go left to reach the road. Go over the level crossing to Shiplake Station.

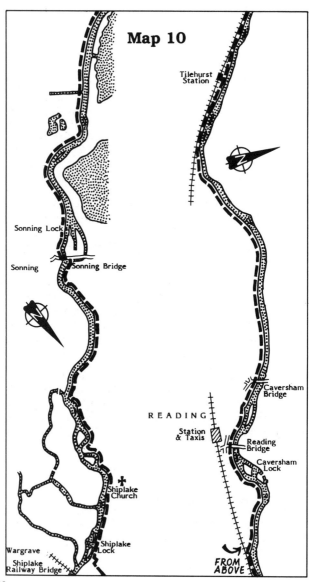

Map 10

Tilehurst Station

Sonning Lock

Sonning Sonning Bridge

Caversham Bridge

READING

Station & Taxis

Reading Bridge

Caversham Lock

Shiplake Church

Wargrave

Shiplake Lock

Shiplake Railway Bridge

FROM ABOVE

SHIPLAKE is such a scattered village that the riverside church is not reached for 1¹/₂ miles. Lashbrook Chapel, a converted barn, serves those living near the station and the village shop. As a child author George Orwell lived at Roselawn (top of Station Road on corner of Quarry Lane). The Thames Path will eventually run through the station to join the towpath which returns to the left bank at former Lashbrook Ferry to provide a view of Wargrave.

The temporary way is ahead up Station Road to pass The Baskerville Arms. At the crossroads turn left along Mill Road for ¹/₂ mile to a postbox (left) at the turning for Lashbrook House and Farm. Once over Lash Brook go right down steps to a stile and bear half left across the corner of the field to a second stile. Here turn right along the field boundary. In winter there is a view (left) of Wargrave Manor up on the hill beyond the river. After a stile a short path runs to a road. Opposite is Mill House. Turn right for a few yards to go left down the path leading to the lock.

SHIPLAKE LOCK The lock island has been a summer campsite since the 1890s - two families being regulars since the 1920s. In summer there is a shop serving teas next to the lock keeper's house. Until 1984 Mill House was the home of Colonel Robert Phillimore who worked the mill. Upstream is Phillimore's Island named after his ancestor Sir Robert Phillimore.

Just before the lock go right over the TC stile by the normally chained TC gate to follow the towpath alongside a meadow. There is another Conservancy gate and a stile before the way becomes enclosed at a stile below Shiplake House. Soon there is a view up through thin trees to Shiplake College. At a wide grass area a path runs uphill to Shiplake Church.

SHIPLAKE CHURCH The south aisle is the original 1140 church. The font is a copy of the one in Iffley Church. The medieval glass is from a French abbey and came here after being buried during the French Revolution. In 1850 the poet Alfred Tennyson was married here and wrote a poem for the vicar in lieu of the fee. Shiplake College was built as a residence in 1905 followed by The White House three years later.

The towpath continues over the high bridge and near the water. There is a distant view (right) of gas holders on the edge of Reading as the way double bends to run through a wood opposite two islands. The path is alongside a series of fields until reaching (at a point a little back from the present bank) a willow and poplar wood near Sonning. Just before the bridge there is an attractive redundant gateway (right) to The French Horn Hotel inland at Sonning Eye. Cross to Sonning Island and turn left over the road bridge passing from Oxfordshire to Berkshire as indicated on the stone in the middle (right) to reach Sonning.

SONNING is pronounced 'sunning' which was still the spelling in the late 18th century. The river was not only the county boundary but also the diocesan boundary between Salisbury and Lincoln. The Bishop of Salisbury had a house here on high ground south-west of the church from 1075 to 1574. Deanery Gardens, an arts and crafts style house designed by Edwin Lutyens and completed in 1902 for *Country Life* editor Edward Hudson, has grounds laid out by Gertrude Jekyll incorporating the Dean of Salisbury's walled garden. The church was founded in Saxon times with the present building dating from 1180. It had a St Siric Chapel which was a place of pilgrimage for the mentally ill - The Bull next to the churchyard was the pilgrim lodging. The bishop maintained a wooden bridge which was succeeded by the present river crossing in 1772. William Morris dined at The White Hart (now The Great House Hotel) during his journey upstream in 1880. Sonning Mill on the island was a working mill until 1969.

Go right along the hard surface towpath to Sonning Lock. (To the south-west of the church there is a path back to the river.) Beyond the lock, the towpath continues alongside trees with a view over to lakes behind the far bank. After a nature reserve sign the path runs out on to a wide expanse of grass. Stay by the river and cross a bridge over a narrow water channel dug for a (demolished) power station. Shortly after the Reading Town Regatta Boathouse the path swings round to the Kennet & Avon Canal entrance. Cross the canal mouth by using Horseshoe Bridge.

HORSESHOE BRIDGE, attached to the 1839 Great Western Railway Brunel railway bridge, dates from the 1890s and has high sides to prevent the towing horses from being frightened at the high crossing. The canal runs to Newbury and Bath.

On the far side the path enters Reading and passes a supermarket where customers can arrive by water. The river curves south round King's Meadow, giving a view of the town with the prison in the foreground, to Caversham Lock - in 1996 the first to have a full-time woman lock-keeper for over a century. Beyond is Reading Bridge.

Refreshments
Henley: The Henley Tea Rooms, Thames-Side (on riverside just upstream of The Angel).

Shiplake (Station end): The Baskerville Arms, Station Road. 12-2.30pm & 6-11pm. (Sun 12-2.30pm & 7-10.30pm).

Sonning: The Tea Cosy, High Street. Open daily for all meals including cream teas (01734 698178).

Sonning: The Bull, next to the churchyard. 11am-3pm & 5.30-11pm. All day at weekends.

Reading: Tesco café, on towpath between Horseshoe Bridge and King's Meadow.

Accommodation
Henley: Lenwade, 3 Western Road, RG9 1JL (01491 573468).

Henley: Avalon, 36 Queen Street, RG9 1AP (01491 577829).

Henley: Swiss Farm campsite (01491 573419). Mar-Oct.Take right fork at end of Bell Street.

Shiplake: The Baskerville Arms, Station Road, RG9 3NY (0118 9403332).

Transport
Henley: Rail (Thames Trains).

Shiplake: Rail (Thames Trains).

Reading: Rail (Thames Trains/Great Western/Virgin Trains/South West Trains).

Tourist Information
Henley: Town Hall, Market Place RG9 2AQ (01491 578034).

Map
OS Landranger 176 (Reading & Windsor).

11. Reading to Pangbourne
7 miles

Reading may have expanded in the last half of the 20th century but the river still provides a pleasant route through the conurbation of Reading, Caversham, Tilehurst and Purley. Pangbourne is reached after a pleasant meadow walk with views of two historic mansions.

READING Abbey, founded in 1121 when stone from France was brought up the Thames and unloaded on the Kennet, attracted many pilgrims to see the hand of St James the Great. Alongside the ruins is a new church built partly with abbey stones just outside the old church's north transept. The Benedictine monastery's closure and partial destruction in 1539 has left Henry I's body buried somewhere under St James's School playground. St Laurence's, part of the abbey precinct, remains intact and here the future Archbishop Laud, son of a Reading draper, was baptised in 1573. Later Jane Austen went to school in the surviving Abbey gateway. In the ruined chapter house are the words and music of the oldest recorded English song *Sumer is icumen in*. The Lady Chapel site is now occupied by the Prison where Oscar Wilde was imprisoned in 1895. Three famous businesses were founded here: Sutton, born in the year of Waterloo, turned his father's corn merchant's into Sutton Seeds; Thomas Huntley, who made biscuits for travellers, teamed up with George Palmer to form Huntley & Palmer's (export biscuits went by barge to London Docks); and hatter Austin Reed opened the first shop in 1900. The railway's arrival had a huge effect on the town which soon became Berkshire's county capital instead of Abingdon. Reading Museum (open Tue-Sat 10am-5pm; Sun 2-5pm; admission free) has a replica of the Bayeux Tapestry and displays on the Abbey.

From Reading Bridge go upstream over the Environment Agency's River Division quay and past Fry's Island.

FRY'S ISLAND, home of the only bowls club in Britain reached by ferry, is known locally as De Montfort Island after a duel fought
104

there in 1163 between Robert de Montfort and Henry Earl of Essex in the presence of Henry II. De Montfort had accused Essex of dropping the Royal Standard during a battle with the Welsh but Essex denied the charge. In the duel watched by thousands Essex fell and his body was taken to Reading Abbey. However, the defeated nobleman was not dead and after recovering from his wounds he joined the community.

Ahead, just past The Riverside pub (on a boatyard site), is Caversham Bridge.

CAVERSHAM BRIDGE is the third here. The first was built about 1219 by Reading Abbey to improve the road to Oxford. On the downstream side, near the Caversham bank where the bridge crosses an island, there was St Anne's Chapel. Relics included the dagger used to murder Henry VI. Stone from the chapel is incorporated into Our Lady of Caversham Chapel built on to Caversham's Our Lady & St Anne Church (South View Avenue) in 1959. On the Reading bank there was the Holy Ghost Chapel which gave way to the White Hart Inn now rebuilt as Three Men in a Boat Tavern. St Anne's Well can be found at the top of Caversham's Priest Hill on the left bank. St Peter's Church, which stands on high ground above gardens and allotments, has a Norman doorway. The nearby Rectory has a riverside garden from where a recent rector dived daily into the Thames every summer for 20 years.

After the bridge and pub there is Reading Rowing Club (Tuck Shop at the back). A clear wide towpath runs along the bank with views of Caversham's church and substantial houses with boathouses.

Later, the way narrows at fields to pass St Mary's Island and cross a former boatyard. The railway comes close to the towpath as it passes Appletree Eyot and Poplar Island. Below Tilehurst Station the reach is known as the Kentwood Deeps. Leave the river at the Beethovens Hotel pub sign to climb steps over the railway whilst the towpath continues for a short distance before switching briefly to the left bank for the bend north.

BEETHOVENS HOTEL was until 1995 The Roebuck. This was the name in 1882 when a 17th-century pub was enlarged to provide for anglers and boatmen - two years later the winning Cambridge Boat Race crew was based here during training. The name Roebuck lives on with Roebuck Ferry Cottage a few yards upstream.

Turn right along the main road to pass a Purley-on-Thames sign level with a strategically placed wartime pill box. Follow the wall by the woodland and at the end turn right down steps leading to residential Skerritt Way. Turn left along the road. Ahead on the hill can be seen Purley Park mansion. At a junction go left again into Hazel Road which passes the entrance to the mansion (Purley Park Trust). At a crossroads go right over the railway and down New Hill.

PURLEY has long presented problems for anyone following the Thames. In the 1780s the Thames Commissioners faced opposition to a towpath from the owner of a riverside meadow and orchard in front of the church. In 1784 two ferries were established to enable the towpath to run on the opposite bank for $^1/_3$ mile. The failure of the Commissioners to carry through a threat of compulsory purchase caused the Countryside Commission much work 200 years later when preparing the Thames Path route. The church (at the eastern end of St Mary's Avenue) has an early 17th-century tower but there has been a church here since Norman times. Purley Park mansion, designed by James Wyatt, was built in 1800 with a parkland embracing the church with the village to the west.

At the bottom of New Hill turn left and right to go up a rough track, Mapledurham Drive. This is the access road for Mapledurham Lock. There is a gate halfway along but just before the cattle grid go ahead over the stile and keep forward. In winter Mapledurham House (on the far bank) can be seen through the trees. At the towpath go right for a short distance only for a good view of Mapledurham Church and House. The Thames Path continues left through a gate to a footbridge leading to Mapledurham Lock.

MAPLEDURHAM HOUSE & LOCK On the left bank is the river's last working mill. The mansion was built in 1588 and remains occupied by the same family. (Neither can be reached on foot from the towpath.) The lock setting inspired some of E.H. Shepard's

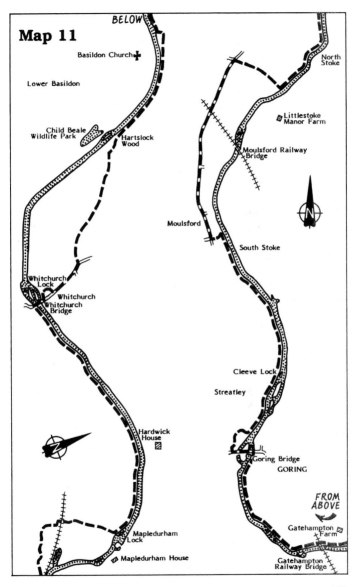

Map 11

BELOW

Basildon Church✝

Lower Basildon

Child Beale Wildlife Park

Hartslock Wood

North Stoke

Littlestoke Manor Farm

Moulsford Railway Bridge

Moulsford

South Stoke

Whitchurch Lock

Whitchurch

Whitchurch Bridge

Cleeve Lock

Streatley

Hardwick House

Goring Bridge
GORING

FROM ABOVE

Gatehampton Farm

Mapledurham Lock

Mapledurham House

Gatehampton Railway Bridge

drawings for *The Wind in the Willows* with Mapledurham House said, among others, to be the artist's model for 'Toad Hall'.

The path continues alongside a meadow passing through several TC gates. Just after TC kissing gate 189 there is a brief view across the water to Hardwick House on the Oxfordshire bank.

HARDWICK HOUSE Elizabeth I visited the mansion soon after completion. Charles I played bowls on the lawn running down to the Thames towards the end of his troubled reign when the house suffered damage in the Civil War. The Tudor house, in the hands of the Lybbe family until the end of the 19th century, is now the residence of Sir Julian Rose who runs the 300 acre Hardwick Organic Farm noted for its unpasteurised milk. His great-grandfather, Sir Charles, was the model for 'Toad' in *Wind in the Willows* and the house is the author Kenneth Grahame's most likely inspiration for 'Toad Hall'.

Inland on this Berkshire bank is Westbury Farm vineyard. Later the towpath passes through National Trust owned Pangbourne Meadow before reaching Whitchurch Bridge.

Refreshments
Caversham Bridge: Three Men in a Boat Tavern. 12-2.30pm & 5.30-11pm.
Caversham Bridge: Tuck Shop at upstream Reading Rowing Club.
Mapledurham Lock: Café open on fine summer days.

Accommodation
Reading: Berkeley Guest House, 32 Berkeley Ave, RG1 6JE (0118 9595699).

Transport
Reading: Rail (Thames Trains/Great Western/Virgin Trains/South West Trains).
Purley: Rail (Thames Trains) from Tilehurst.
Pangbourne: Rail (Thames Trains).

Tourist Information
Reading: Town Hall, Blagrave Street, RG1 1QH (0118 9566226).

Map
OS Landranger 176 (Reading & Windsor).

Narrowboat near Goring

12. Pangbourne to Goring
4 miles

At Whitchurch there is the Thames Path's longest diversion from the riverside and the only steep climb. This is because the towpath stays on the right bank until Gatehampton where the ferry has ceased to operate. The high walk is in woodland with views down on to the towpath before the river turns north to Goring Gap.

PANGBOURNE is named after the River Pang which joins the Thames here. The village sign incorporates a copy of *The Wind in the Willows* by Kenneth Grahame who lived at Church Cottage, with the old village lock-up in the garden, from 1924 until his death in 1932. His funeral was at the next door church decorated with willows gathered that morning from the river. The St James the Less dedication may have originally been 'the Great' since the church belonged to Reading Abbey whose abbot had a house here. The tower was built in 1718 and the main church rebuilt in the 1860s. The Angel Gabriel in the west window featured on a 1992 Christmas stamp. D.H. Evans, founder of the department store, lived at Shooters Hill House (now the Masonic Hall) and built in 1896 the so-called 'Seven Deadly Sins' - the houses facing the river upstream of The Swan. Malicious local gossip maintained that they were for Evans' mistresses. One occupant was society hostess Lady Cunard.

Cross the bridge from Berkshire to Oxfordshire to enter Whitchurch-on-Thames.

WHITCHURCH BRIDGE Although there was a ferry here the river could be forded until the 1790s when the channel was dredged to accommodate barges from the new Thames & Severn Canal. The first bridge, steep and wooden, was built in 1792. The present iron bridge opened in 1902 and is one of only two Thames bridges maintaining tolls. Pedestrians, sheep, boars and pigs used to be charged $^1/_2$d each. Carriages were 2d "for each and every wheel" and today cars are charged 8p but since decimalization walkers cross free.

WHITCHURCH The mill is mentioned in Domesday Book. The church also dates from Norman times but is now largely Victorian - a north aisle window shows Jesus at work with a saw in his stepfather's workshop. Nearby is a monument to Richard Lybbe of Hardwick. The long main street has a pub but the village lost its independence when the Post Office, which sold everything from food to haberdashery, closed recently.

Before the Whitchurch-on-Thames sign go left to enter the driveway to The Mill. To the left there is a view across the water to the bridge. Beyond the cottage turn right up a walled footpath running under a vine to the churchyard. Beyond the lychgate keep forward to return to the road.

Turn left to pass The Greyhound. The street climbs the hill and just beyond the former shop (left) the pavement ends. Keep on past the White House (left) to turn left where signs point to Long Acre Farm and Public Bridleway to Goring.

Follow the track for $^1/_2$ mile to where the way bends left to Hartslock Farm. Here continue ahead down a stepped path into a

valley. **The enclosed path climbs up between fields. On entering Hartslock Wood follow a winding path which is later briefly along the edge of a chalk cliff with a sheer drop - the only such experience on the Thames Path. This affords the first good view of the river and islands.**

HARTSLOCK WOOD is named after the former Hart's Lock which was at the two islands below. There may have been a flash lock here as early as the 12th century. The name comes from a river family.

The woodland path continues along a shelf on the hillside. As the path descends through the beech trees and old yews there are more river views. Across the water is the towpath and Basildon Church.

BASILDON The 13th-century church with a 1734 tower stands alone except for a farm. Agriculturalist Jethro Tull is buried in the churchyard. Here the river is rich in wildlife due to the Child-Beale Wildlife Trust to the east by the towpath.

Where the ground levels out the path becomes enclosed as it runs along the side of a field. Here the path is a little way from the river but just before reaching a tall hedge at Gatehampton Farm turn left on to a side path. Beyond a backwater bridge is Ferry Cottage (left).

GATEHAMPTON Here the towpath comes over from the Basildon bank. This spot has been under almost continuous occupation. Stone Age relics have been discovered and the earliest evidence of post-glacial man in Britain has been found near the railway which cuts through the site of a Roman grain drier.

Turn right to follow the towpath to an open field. Go under the bridge and after some distance through a kissing gate. The Goring Gap hills can be seen half right. As the ground indicates, many walkers cut the corner although the towpath stays with the riverbank. After a stile the towpath leaves the fields and passes three well spaced and charming boathouses. Soon there is a view of Streatley Bridge before the path passes the old ferry point (grass picnic area) and the moorings from where there is a view of the large Ferry Cottage and Goring Church. Cross the mill stream

to reach Goring Bridge.

Refreshments

Pangbourne: Ducks Ditty, Reading Road. 10am-5pm; 7-12pm (closed Sun).

Pangbourne: The Coffee Pot, High Street. 9am-5.30pm (closed Tue & Sun afternoon).

Accommodation

Pangbourne: Weir View House, Shooters Hill, RG8 7BJ (0118 9842120).

Whitchurch: The Rectory, RG8 7DF (0118 9843219).

Transport

Pangbourne: Rail (Thames Trains).

Goring: Rail (Thames Trains) from Goring & Streatley.

Maps

OS Landranger 175 (Reading & Windsor) and 174 (Newbury).

13. Goring to Wallingford

7 miles

This stretch has both the shortest and the longest reach between locks. At Goring the river comes out of the long gorge into a plateau rich in wildfowl. Runsford Hole is the first of two holes in this chapter - hole means 'a place where water is deep'.

GORING The Norman church, later dedicated to St Thomas à Becket, was part of a convent - corbels on the south outside wall supported a cloister roof. Inside a bell dates from about 1290 and the rood screen from just 1912 is made of wood from HMS *Thunderer* in Nelson's fleet. Oscar Wilde spent the summer of 1893 at Ferry Cottage and his play *An Ideal Husband* includes references to the area, such as 'Viscount Goring' and 'Countess Basildon'. The cottage was later enlarged to become the home of Sir Arthur 'Bomber' Harris who died here in 1984. The mill, mentioned in Domesday Book, is the subject of an unfinished painting by J.M.W. Turner. Napper's grocers has been in the same family for over a century.

Cross the bridge to leave Oxfordshire and reach Streatley on the Berkshire bank.

STREATLEY BRIDGE Since the ancient Ridgeway (or Icknield Way from The Wash to Wiltshire) crosses here there must have been a ford from early times. A ferry was running from at least Henry I's time but the river continued to be forded until 1797 when the building of Goring Lock raised the water level. This made the ferry crossing more dangerous and there were deaths when the ferry boat overturned in 1810. The first bridge opened in 1838 with a tollgate on the central island. The present bridge dates from 1923.

STREATLEY means 'road' referring to the Ridgeway. In the 1830s Moses Saunders, the last ferryman, was innkeeper at The Swan. His boat building business eventually moved to Cowes to become the famous Saunders-Rowe. The Swan, although on the Berkshire bank, is partly in Oxfordshire because the mill, which stood across the road, belonged to Goring's convent. The church was rebuilt in the 13th century by Bishop Poore of Salisbury who was responsible for his new cathedral and its spire but here the tower was added 200 years later. Streatley House in the main street dates from about 1765 and was home of the Morrell family - relatives of the Bloomsbury Group's Lady Ottoline.

Turn right to the church to continue round a double bend. Beyond the cottages keep right of the gate ahead to follow the narrow path which soon bears right along a causeway and through a towpath gate.

STREATLEY TO GATE was replaced by the National Rivers Authority (NRA). It is rare to see a Conservancy or NRA gate inland but this inland path is the towpath. Towing horses were led over the bridge and along this route whilst their barges were poled across the river.

Cross a low footbridge and bear round to the left to find a gate by the river. Beyond another gate the towpath crosses a draw-bridge at an inlet. Soon the path converges with the track to Cleeve Lock.

CLEEVE LOCK On the far bank is the 17th-century four bedroom Cleeve Mill which generates its own electricity.

Soon there is a view across to The Leatherne Bottel below a cliff.

THE LEATHERNE BOTTEL was popular in the 16th and 17th centuries for its water from a spring which had been known to the Romans. The pub is now a noted restaurant where diners have included celebrities such as Lord Jenkins, Emma Thompson, Kenneth Branagh, Rula Lenska, George Cole, Willie Carson and Keith Floyd. Its garden supplies herbs and vegetables.

Later the towpath is through a willow copse at Runsford Hole to pass out of Berkshire into Oxfordshire (but still Berkshire until 1974). Soon after there is a view of South Stoke Church beyond the far bank. The way is alongside a wood before reaching the mooring at The Beetle & Wedge at Moulsford.

THE BEETLE & WEDGE, a riverside hotel, is on a former timber wharf. A 'beetle' is a mallet used for driving a wedge into logs for splitting before being floated downstream. This is 'The Potwell Inn' in H.G. Wells' *History of Mr Polly* which he wrote here. It also features in Jerome's *Three Men in a Boat*. Bernard Shaw often stayed when the landlord ran the ferry for the towpath which switches banks here. In the early 19th century it cost $1^{1/2}$d to take a towing horse across. At the end of the century water was so low one summer that carts laden with the harvest forded here as they must have done when Moulsford was a 'mules ford'. The abandoned ferry occasionally reopens in the summer.

Turn inland between the pub buildings to walk up Ferry Lane to a crossroads. Ahead is Moulsford village shop. Turn right along the main road.

MOULSFORD Next to the Manor House is the small church by George Gilbert Scott built in 1846 on the site of a 12th-century church. Upstream Moulsford Preparatory School at the north end of the village opened in 1961.

The Thames Path will eventually return to the river opposite Offlands Farm but until the path is open continue along the main road and across the Paddington-Oxford railway line to a cross- roads beyond a terrace of houses. Turn right down Papist Way to rejoin the river at Littlestoke Ferry which brings the towpath back to the Moulsford bank. Turn left upstream along the towpath which, whilst in the nature reserve, tends to run a little away from the bank to cut a corner. There are several redundant gateways before the path is level with North Stoke on the left bank.

NORTH STOKE village, $1/2$ mile upstream from the old ferry, is almost hidden. The church tower was built in 1725 but at the base are medieval wall paintings. Its dedication is St Mary of Bec following the wedding there of a local Saxon lord to a Norman baron's daughter. The 17th-century Rectory Farmhouse was recently the home of actor Michael Caine who was born downstream at Rotherhithe.

Soon after a gateway by a wood the path is over several gardens. Afterwards Wittenham Clumps can be seen half left

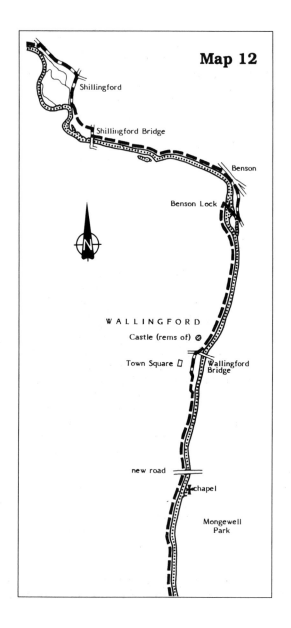

Map 12

Shillingford

Shillingford Bridge

Benson

Benson Lock

WALLINGFORD

Castle (rems of)

Town Square

Wallingford
Bridge

new road

chapel

Mongewell
Park

before the path draws level with Mongewell Park opposite.

MONGEWELL PARK came into the hands of Shute Barrington in 1770, a year after he became Bishop of Llandaff. He was translated to Salisbury before becoming, for 35 years until his death in 1826, Bishop of Durham. He had married the daughter of the previous owner Sir John Guise. The Georgian mansion was demolished in 1890 but the chapel, where the Bishop is buried, survives by the river - upstream of the inlet. In winter the estate's ice house would be filled with at least 20 cart loads of ice from the Thames. The modern buildings were part of Carmel College, the Jewish school, founded in 1948 and closed in 1997.

Soon after the Path passes under the 1993 Wallingford by-pass bridge. At Chalmore Hole the tow-path is suddenly enclosed.

CHALMORE HOLE is the site of Wallingford Lock which existed from 1838 to 1883. It was only used at times of very low water and so was usually

Thames Path's entry into Wallingford

117

left open. Jerome in *Three Men in a Boat* is confused when he fails to find the lock. The Thames Conservancy building on the left is a reminder of the lock which was by the far bank with the weir just below Bradford's Brook crossed here. The Path ahead is now a footpath whilst the towpath continues on the left bank - a ferry was introduced after the lock's removal.

Continue over a boatyard and ahead through a break in the hedge. At Lower Wharf go round a bend and at once turn right to go under an archway in a house and over the mill stream. A path runs behind Wallingford's St Leonard's Church. Turn right along Thames Street to reach the main road. The town centre is to the left but the Thames Path continues to the right to Wallingford Bridge.

Refreshments

Goring: Riverside Tea Rooms, Bridge Approach. Speciality: Thames Banana Barge ice cream. 10am-8pm (6pm Nov-Mar).

Accommodation

Goring: The John Barleycorn, Manor Road, RG8 9DP (01491 872509).

Goring: Miller of Mansfield, High Street, RG8 9AW (01491 872829).

Goring: Leyland Guesthouse, 3 Wallingford Rd, RG8 0AX (01491 872119). Easter-Oct.

Goring: 14 Mountfield, Wallingford Rd, RG8 0BE (01491 872029).

Streatley: YHA, Reading Road, RG8 9JJ (01491 872278).

Moulsford: White House, OX10 9JD (01491 651397).

Transport

Goring: Rail (Thames Trains) to Goring & Streatley.

Moulsford: Rail (Thames Trains) from Cholsey (turn left at Papist Way crossroads).

Wallingford: Bus to Cholsey (Reading Buses 105) then rail (Thames Trains). On certain days there are trains from Wallingford to Cholsey Station (information 01491 835067).

Maps

OS Landranger 175 (Reading & Windsor) and 174 (Newbury).

Shillingford Court at Shillingford Wharf

14. Wallingford to Dorchester
5 miles

This is a short walk by way of Benson and Shillingford to reach the confluence of the Thames and Thame beneath the Sinodun Hills. Nearby is Dorchester, dominated by its huge church, where the monastic guesthouse maintains the tradition of hospitality by serving teas.

WALLINGFORD, meaning 'Welsh people's ford', is on the London-Wales road. A chamberlain appointed annually is in charge of the bridge dating from the 13th century. There was both a wooden bridge and a ford when William the Conqueror crossed here in 1066 on his journey from Hastings to London. Next year he ordered the building of the castle where later Chaucer's son was Constable. The castle, open in summer, was reduced to its ruined state in 1646 by Cromwell after a 16 week siege. The George & Dragon, dating from

119

1517, has tears drawn on a wall by a landlord's daughter who saw her Royalist soldier fiancé stabbed in the bar. The town once had eleven parish churches. The redundant St Peter's with its candle snuffer steeple was designed by Sir Robert Taylor in 1777 although some suggest that jurist Sir William Blackstone who lived at riverside Castle Priory suggested the tower. Today the town has Judge Stephen Tumin as its High Steward. The Market Place is dominated by the 1670 Town Hall in front of St Mary-le-More from where a curfew is rung. The weekly Friday market dates from an 1155 Henry I charter - the 1153 Treaty of Wallingford had confirmed the Plantagenet succession. William Morris stayed at The Town Arms in 1880 on his trip between houses. Artist George Dunlop Leslie lived at Riverside in Thames Street from 1884 to 1907. Actress Sheila Hancock was taught to swim in the Thames when a young wartime evacuee.

At Wallingford Bridge turn down Castle Lane at the side of The Town Arms. Go right at the back of Mill House Restaurant to reach the towpath. Soon there is a view across to the Institute of Hydrology. Later the towpath is so eroded that the way continues, beyond a stile, on the inside of the iron fence. After a couple of stiles look out for the gap in the fence in order to reach Benson Lock. Cross the downstream gates and walk over the weir and a new millstream bridge on the far bank.

Go up to a gate at the road and turn left. At a junction, where is a view of Benson Church, go ahead and when the houses end turn left into a riverside park where the towpath returns at a former ferry point. Go through the gate to reach Benson Cruiser Station on the edge of Benson.

BENSON The partly Norman church was under Dorchester Abbey until 1534. The clock added in 1794 is said to have come from Horse Guards in Whitehall. During the Civil War Charles I held a Privy Council meeting at The Red Lion, now Monarch Court House private residence. Benson, once called Bensington, was on the edge of marshland - the footpath alongside Ferry Road is called the High Path since the river used to flood the road. On the riverside are recorded the distances to London Bridge (92 miles) and Cricklade (63 miles).

Continue through the boatyard to pass a caravan park. Soon the towpath is alongside meadows with a view of the riverside garden wall of Rush Court on the far bank. Later the towpath is by a fence as it approaches Shillingford Bridge with a view of the hotel.

SHILLINGFORD BRIDGE, one of the finest on the river, is exactly halfway between Reading and Oxford and Windsor and Lechlade. There was probably a short-lived wooden bridge here in the 14th century. Another wooden structure was thrown across in the 1780s. The present balustraded stone crossing was built in 1827. The Shillingford Bridge Hotel was once The Swan Inn welcoming "rowing and picnic parties". The 'Shilling-ford' was probably Roman and upstream beyond Shillingford Wharf.

At the bridge go inland to climb up to the road. Leave the towpath (which crosses the bridge) and opposite Ferry House turn left down a road marked 'private' at the side of Bridge House. At High Trees keep right. Go right through the kissing gate at the side to follow a narrow enclosed path. Just beyond Shillingford Court turn left along a short passage to Shillingford Wharf.

SHILLINGFORD WHARF was once used by a brewery (opposite The Kingfisher at the far end of the road) and coal was landed here for Warborough to the north. In the 1980s *Church Times* editor John Whale undertook an annual August swim from here to Shillingford Bridge. The towpath is on the far bank and crosses back upstream at the former Keen Edge Ferry. 'Keen' comes from 'cane' meaning 'willows'. W.B. Yeats stayed at Wheeler's End (timber-framed on west side of road north of crossroads) in summer 1921 whilst beginning the poem *Meditations in Time of Civil War*.

Walk the length of Wharf Road to the crossroads by The Kingfisher. Turn left along the main road - at the bus stop it is necessary to cross over to follow the pavement from where there is soon an early view of Dorchester Abbey. Once past the solitary house look out for a gateway on the left, just opposite the huge traffic sign.

Cross the road with care to go through the kissing gate and ahead to rejoin the towpath which crossed back at Keen Edge

Ferry. Turn right to continue upstream. Later the towpath crosses the River Thame entrance at a gated bridge.

RIVER THAME rises just north of Aylesbury in Buckinghamshire. The river's sheltered entrance is a popular mooring although it is difficult to sail as far as Dorchester. It was in the Thame near here that St Birinus baptised King Cynegils of Wessex. Some have insisted that 'Thames' comes from an amalgamation of 'Thame' and 'Isis'. The latter is the Oxford name for the Thames. Others simply say that from this confluence to just beyond Oxford the river is the 'Isis' rather than 'Thames'. This may derive from Thamesis, the Latin for Thames.

Beyond the bridge a path runs inland towards a stile and on to nearby Dorchester whilst the Thames Path continues on the towpath with Little Wittenham Wood on the far bank.

Refreshments

Wallingford: Annie's Tea Rooms, 79 High Street (01491 836308). No smoking tearoom open 10am-5pm except Sun & Wed (but open for Sun tea Jul-Sep).

Wallingford: Harvest Bakery & Café, Market Place. Open weekdays.

Benson: Cruiser station café. Open daily (also laundrette).

Shillingford: The Kingfisher.

Accommodation

Wallingford: The Nook, 2 Thames St, OX10 0BH (01491 834214).

Wallingford: Munts Mill, Castle Lane, OX10 0BN (01491 836654).

Wallingford campsites on Crowmarsh bank: May-Sep (01865 341035) or Feb-Dec (01491 836860).

Benson: Camping Park, OX10 6SJ (01491 838304). Mar-Oct.

Shillingford Bridge: North Farm, Shillingford Hill, OX10 8NB (01865 858406). No smoking. Cross the bridge and turn right for $3/4$ mile.

Shillingford: Marsh House, Court Drive, OX10 7ER (01865 858496). (Turn right by Shillingford Court before Wharf.)

Transport

Wallingford: Rail (Thames Trains) to Cholsey then bus (Reading Buses 105). On certain days there are trains from Cholsey to Wallingford (information 01491 835067).

Dorchester: Bus (Reading Buses 105) to Oxford or Cholsey then Rail (Thames Trains).

Tourist Information

Wallingford: Town Hall, Market Place, OX10 0EG (01491 826972).

Maps

OS Landranger 175 (Reading & Windsor) and 164 (Oxford).

15. Dorchester to Abingdon

9 miles

DORCHESTER-on-Thames was once Dorchester-on-Thame after the river which runs close to the Roman town. The 12th-century abbey church replaced a Saxon cathedral founded by St Birinus who baptised King Cynegils of Wessex in the Thame. The abbey has a 14th-century wall painting, a sculptured Jesse window and the restored St Birinus shrine. The guest house is now a popular tea rooms and the abbey brewhouse has become The George Hotel - one of ten inns in the 18th century serving the Oxford-London coaches. On the path to the Thames is St Birinus' Church which was built in 1849 to a design by Pugin follower William Wilkinson Wardell whose other work includes Melbourne Cathedral.

(Route out of Dorchester to river: Leave the abbey church by the south gate, next to the the toll-house, and bear left. Just before the bridge go left to find a hidden path which runs down to a tunnel. Once through the low passage turn left to pass St Birinus' Church.

Continue ahead to keep on the right side of the green. Keep forward but before reaching a thatched cottage ahead go sharp right under a barrier and up a short path. At the end go left and where the way divides keep forward [but not directly ahead] on a footpath running down the side of a field. Go over a wooden stile at the end to continue south. Stay near the field boundary to the left to bear round the corner of the oddly shaped field and find a stile ahead. Still continue forward to meet the River Thame at a bend and follow the bank to its confluence with the Thames.)

Where the Rivers Thame and Thames meet take the Thames Path upstream with Little Wittenham Wood to the left on the far bank. Soon the Thames turns north to Day's Lock beneath Little Wittenham.

LITTLE WITTENHAM The church, which has a 15th-century tower, was once a daughter church of Abingdon Abbey. Opposite a path

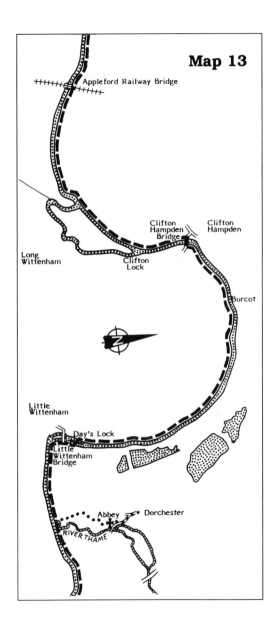

Map 13

Appleford Railway Bridge

Clifton
Hampden
Bridge

Clifton
Hampden

Long
Wittenham

Clifton
Lock

Burcot

Little
Wittenham

Day's Lock

Little
Wittenham
Bridge

Abbey

Dorchester

RIVER THAME

Thames Conservancy gate near Day's Lock

leads up to Wittenham Clumps on the Sinodun Hills - the local name is 'Mother Daunch's Buttocks' after Oliver Cromwell's aunt who lived at The Manor House next to the church. The beech trees are partly in an Iron Age fort. Artist Paul Nash first drew the Clumps in 1912 and his later oil version, *Landscape of the Vernal Equinox*, is in the Queen Mother's collection at Clarence House. The bridge to the hamlet is the scene of the annual World Pooh Sticks Championships which has been held at noon on the first Sunday in January since 1984 - apart from 1997 when the river was frozen. Upstream Day's Lock acquired its name in the 1820s from a lock-keeper.

126

After passing under the bridge keep ahead to find a kissing gate at the far end of the lock compound. Here the Thames Path crosses the upstream lock gates and the weir to the right bank. (Meanwhile the historic towpath continues on the left bank for a few more yards to a former ferry point at the end of the earthwork.)

The Thames Path joins the line of the towpath as the river begins a long arch westwards round the edge of water meadows grazed by cattle. On the way the path has a view across to Burcot on the far bank.

BURCOT is easily missed on the far side of the Thames behind long gardens but until 1636 this was, due to shallow water and a hard sandstone river bed, the end of navigation where passengers and goods took to the road for Oxford and beyond. There is evidence of Roman occupation here. Back garden views include Burcot Grange and the hotel with its old boathouse.

On approaching Clifton Hampden there is, level with the stile, a lonely cross on the far bank and soon after a view of Clifton Manor. In its garden are two heads - Marlborough and Prince Eugene - mounted on columns. Cross the bridge.

CLIFTON HAMPDEN The village owes its thatched look and bridge to Lord Aldenham, future Governor of the Bank of England, who inherited the village in 1842. The water was so shallow here that cattle were driven across the ferry point and in 1826 the Lord Mayor's barge became stuck on returning from Oxford. When the building of the upstream lock in 1835 raised the level, the ferry (run by Oxford's Exeter College since 1493) was replaced in 1864 by the bridge built of local brick and designed by George Gilbert Scott who had sketched a plan on his starched shirt cuff. He also remodelled the church dating from at least 1180. The Manor House, also on the cliff, is Scott's vicarage. The Barley Mow on the right bank features in Jerome's *Three Men in a Boat* as "the quaintest, most old-world inn up the river". Tolls continued to be collected at the bridge in person by the two nieces of Lord Aldenham until 1946.

Go through the TC gate at the side of the bridge and follow the towpath down to Clifton Lock at the start of Clifton Cut.

CLIFTON CUT, opened in 1822 following the success of the upstream Culham Cut, bypasses straggling Long Wittenham which is reached only by way of Clifton Hampden Bridge. The lock often has postcards and secondhand books on sale in aid of Long Wittenham's mainly 13th-century church.

The towpath continues along Clifton Cut whilst the Old Thames meanders south. Beyond the weir at the end of the cut, the path is uneven with much erosion as it runs alongside fields. After a copse the river passes under the Paddington-Oxford railway. There are now views south to Didcot Power Station and Wittenham Clumps. On approaching Culham the way rises to run through trees. Beyond a stile the towpath briefly joins a wide grass way but soon after a gateway moves from the main path to stay near the water where there is a view of the old river turning south towards Sutton Bridge and Sutton Courtenay. Ahead is Culham Bridge at the start of Culham Cut.

Bablock Hythe Ferry
Ford at Duxford

Ashton Keynes
Looking downstream from Thames Source

CULHAM CUT was opened in 1809 to avoid the tortuous route through Sutton Courtenay to the south. Sutton Bridge replaced a ferry in 1811.

(For alternative route through Sutton Courtenay see below.)

The Thames Path continues over the road approach to Culham Bridge to reach Culham Lock at the start of Culham Cut. Beyond the next bridge (where walkers from Sutton Courtenay rejoin the main route) there is a fine view of Culham.

CULHAM The Manor House, which once belonged to Abingdon Abbey, has a 1685 dovecot near the river. The church is now largely Victorian although the tower was rebuilt earlier in 1710. Until around 1400 the village spread over the field to the west with streets and passageways leading down to the river on two sides.

Where the present village ends the towpath crosses the abutment of an old bridge. As the Old Thames joins from the south and the cut ends the river turns sharply north. At the end of the open field cross a footbridge, guarded by stiles, spanning the entrance to the Swift Ditch.

SWIFT DITCH was cut by Abingdon Abbey in 1052. 'Swift' means 'short cut'. The $1^{1}/2$ mile cut was the main navigation channel until 1550 and again from 1635 to 1790. Barges moored overnight in specially dug pools. The island created by the cut is known as Aldersey Island after St Andrew's Church which stood on it. The 1416 bridge, carrying the main road until 1928, is just upstream from the southern end.

The towpath is alongside the meadows opposite Abingdon with fine views of the confluence with the River Ock and St Helen's with its almshouses before Abingdon Bridge is reached.

Refreshments

Dorchester: Abbey Tea Rooms. Open Wed, Thu & weekends (summer only) from 3pm "until food gone". Good value homemade food. Well behaved dogs admitted. Smokers "evicted immediately".

Clifton Hampden: The Barley Mow, Right Bank. Chef & Brewer meals. 11am-11pm (Sun 12-10.30pm).

Clifton Hampden: The Plough in village. Meals, teas & coffee all day.

Culham: The Lion Inn. Bar snacks. Open basic hours and often all day summer weekends.

Sutton Courtenay: The New Inn, High Street.

Sutton Courtenay: The Fish. Opposite entry into village. 12-3pm & 6-11pm (Sun 7-10.30pm)

Accommodation

Little Wittenham: Rooks Orchard, OX14 4QY (01865 407765).

Clifton Hampden: camping at Bridge House Caravan Site, Bridge House, OX14 3EH (01865 407725).

Sutton Courtenay: Bekynton House, 7 The Green, OX14 4AE (01235 848630).

Transport

Dorchester: Rail (Thames Trains) to Oxford or Cholsey then bus (Reading Buses 105). Stagecoach Oxford.

Abingdon: Bus (Stagecoach, Oxford 24hr service or Oxford Bus Company) to Oxford then Rail (Thames Trains/Great Western/ Virgin Trains).

Map

OS Landranger 164 (Oxford).

Sutton Courtenay Diversion

To follow the old route through Sutton Courtenay turn left over Culham Bridge and at the cottages cross the road to go through a kissing gate on the right. The path follows the Old Thames until the water becomes hidden by a hedge. At a stile go ahead down a drive and over a stile opposite The Fish in the village.

SUTTON COURTENAY Sutton was given to the de Courtenay family in the Norman period. There is Norman Hall near the church. The present Manor House is the seat of the Honourable David Astor, former editor and director of *The Observer*. The Abbey, now a retreat house, was a grange belonging to Abingdon Abbey. Lord Asquith, the last Liberal Prime Minister, lived at The Wharf and is buried in the churchyard along with author George Orwell (Eric Blair; near the far right corner). The Wharf recalls the time when barges called here, passing through a lock by a now disappeared mill, before the Cut was made.

The exit from the village is along to the right just beyond the wall post box at the corner. The path crosses a series of weir bridges. Beyond the main and last crossing bear half right across fields to a bridge spanning the lock cut. Ahead is Culham with Abingdon's St Helen's Church in the distance. Cross the bridge to rejoin the towpath and Thames Path. Turn left.

16. Abingdon to Oxford

9¹/₂ miles

This is a lonely stretch and until recently it was inaccessible from Abingdon. Around Radley the college oarsmen flash past rushes harvested every July for chair seating by Tony Handley of Country Chairmen who is the only supplier of native freshwater rushes. Salisbury Cathedral's chairs have Thames rush seats. The same patch is cut only every three years so sometimes the team of around fourteen harvesters camp as far upstream as Tadpole or Rushey above Oxford. The towpath becomes firmer and busier on approaching Oxford where there is, of course, more rowing.

ABINGDON is one of the oldest continuously inhabited towns in Britain. The Benedictine abbey was here from 695 until 1538. The abbey church has disappeared but some monastic buildings remain at the end of Thames Street which runs parallel with the Abbey Stream dug in the 10th century. Upper Reaches Hotel was the mill house. The gateway is beside St Nicholas' Church which was the Abbey's church for the laity. Outside is a plaque in honour of Abingdon-born St Edmund of Abingdon who became Archbishop of Canterbury in 1233. St Helen's by the river has a 14th-century Lady Chapel ceiling with fine examples of medieval iconography - surviving both the Reformation and Cromwell because it was too high to reach. One of the three adjoining almshouse blocks dates from 1446. Monday has been market day since 1086. County Hall, built between 1678 and 1682 by Christopher Kempster, Wren's master mason at St Paul's, recalls that this was Berkshire's county town until 1867. Morland Brewery was founded here in 1711. MG cars (Morris Garages) were manufactured here from 1929 until 1980. The Michaelmas Fair (Mon-Tues before 11 Oct) is Europe's longest street fair - the smaller Runaway Fair a week later has its origins in the chance for labour hired at the main fair to seek another employer.

Start at the meadows end of Abingdon Bridge opposite the

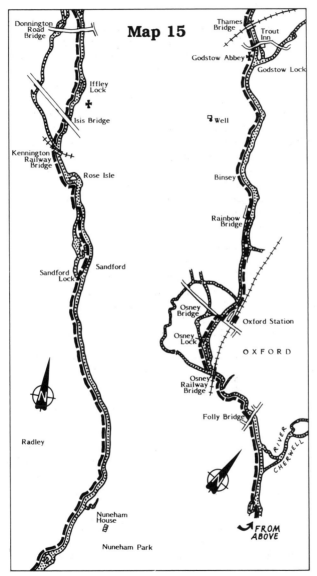

Map 15

Donnington Road Bridge

Thames Bridge

Trout Inn

Godstow Abbey

Godstow Lock

Iffley Lock

Isis Bridge

Well

Kennington Railway Bridge

Rose Isle

Binsey

Rainbow Bridge

Sandford

Sandford Lock

Osney Bridge

Oxford Station

Osney Lock

OXFORD

N

Osney Railway Bridge

Folly Bridge

RIVER CHERWELL

Radley

FROM ABOVE

Nuneham House

Nuneham Park

133

town. Follow the towpath (which runs under the bridge) to reach a gate at Abingdon Lock. Leave the towpath by crossing over the lower lock gates, the lock island and the weir to reach the Abingdon bank.

Follow the Abbey Stream (right) to go over a wooden bridge. At a path junction go right. The path follows a ditch (right). Soon after crossing to the opposite side, the path curves round a long inlet. Bear right (ignoring a permissive path to the left) and at another fork go left. Soon the trees to the right fall away to reveal the river shortly before the point where the towpath switches from the far side. There is a view of the Swift Ditch weir and entrance and St Helen's spire in Abingdon.

The path tread is a little away from the bank both before and after Nuneham Railway Bridge. The way becomes briefly enclosed as it passes Lock Wood Island.

LOCK WOOD ISLAND may not be natural as there was a lock here from at least Elizabethan times until early in the 19th century. The lock channel was by the left bank although the main channel is now on the right by the towpath. This was a popular spot with the thatched lock cottage becoming a tearoom and reached by a rustic bridge. The lonely Old Boathouse residence above the island is the original late 19th-century Radley College Dry Boathouse.

Passing the Old Boathouse frontage there is a framed view of Newnham and soon to the right can be seen the Carfax Conduit up on a wooded hill.

NEWNHAM was 'New Ham'. The riverside was landscaped in the 1770s by 'Capability' Brown when the core of the house was built for the 1st Lord Harcourt. The nearby temple style building is a church designed by Harcourt. The Carfax Conduit stood in Oxford as part of the water supply system from 1615 to 1786. Author Lewis Carroll organised river trips to here from Oxford for picnics in the woods when the party included the original Alice. More recently the house was used by the University.

After another fenced stretch the path is beside fields as far as Radley College Boathouse where a bridge carries the towpath over the slipway.

RADLEY lies a mile inland where there is a station and a pub. St James the Great Church has a Tudor west window showing Henry VII in hunting clothes - the vicarage on the north side was the hunting lodge used by the King. The pulpit canopy is said to come from the House of Commons' Speaker's Chair having been presented by Speaker Lenthall. The Community of the Resurrection (now at Mirfield) was founded here in 1892 by Charles Gore who was Vicar. Radley College was founded in 1847 and old boys include cricketer Captain Ted Dexter and comedian Peter Cook whose mimicry of masters amused contemporaries.

There are more fields and TC gates. After the third gate the path approaches Sandford Lock where a footbridge crosses the wide weir channel to the lock. On the far side is a housing block replacing the mill and The King's Arms.

SANDFORD In 1240 Thomas de Saunford gave the manor to the Knights Templar whose preceptory remains just north of the village on the left bank. The partly Norman church is on high ground nearby. A mill operated here from 1294 until 1982 having in its last years produced coloured paper. The King's Arms site has been an inn since the 15th century. The lock is the deepest on the river and one of the oldest. Among those who drowned in the fierce 'Sandford Lasher' weir upstream was the original Peter Pan, Michael Llewelyn Davies.

The towpath continues beyond a TC gate and just as the way becomes enclosed there is a view of Sandford Church tower. The towpath crosses two weir bridges before continuing along an island. A little further on the towpath bears left to cross the weir stream mouth. After a second TC gate there is a choice of paths for whilst the towpath remains faithful to the river there is a public footpath cutting the corner. The river double bends at Rose Isle.

ROSE ISLE was known in the 19th century as both St Michael's Island and Kennington Island after the village behind the railway on the right bank. The present house replaced The Swan Inn.

After the two paths have merged there is evidence of two inlets - one missing a bridge. Keep ahead to go through a gate at a railway bridge.

KENNINGTON RAILWAY BRIDGE carried the Oxford-High Wycombe branch line opened in 1864. Now the track runs only as far as Cowley. The present bridge was built in 1923 immediately downstream of the old abutments. The new Hinksey towpath bridge immediately upstream, crossing the long weirstream, replaces a 1920s structure.

The towpath is now alongside a wood before passing under Isis Bridge (road 1962) to find Iffley Lock ahead. By the path are the Iffley Meadows and soon there is a view of Iffley Church across the water.

IFFLEY The origin of the name is uncertain. The church is an outstanding Norman example built about 1170. The stone decoration has links with sculpture once found at Reading Abbey and a doorway has flowers found elsewhere only in the cathedral porch at Santiago de Compostela. Recent sensitive interior changes at Iffley Church include in 1995 replacing Victorian glass with a John Piper design. Until the middle of the 20th century funeral processions came by river - bodies could not be carried over the lock for fear of creating a right of way. The mill was burnt down in 1908 but some mill stones remain outside Grist Cottage and Mill House Garden in Mill Lane by the weir. The lock is one of the oldest pound locks dating from 1632 and rebuilt in 1923 with rollers (by the towpath) for punts.

Just round the corner on the towpath there is the The Isis pub.

THE ISIS was built as a farmhouse in about 1800 and became an inn in 1842. The interior is decorated with plenty of oars and there is a skittle alley. Until 1979 beer was delivered by punt. Artist Peter de Wint (1784-1849) painted the view a little upstream from the towpath of the inn with Iffley Church in the background. The house's surrounding farmland is wet meadowland noted for rare snake's head fritillaries flowering in late spring. Also found here are adder's tongue fern, common meadow rue and marsh marigold.

At the end of the meadow the towpath runs under Donnington Bridge (road 1926). St John's College barge may be moored in a backwater on the far side. Soon after passing the Oxford City

boundary stone, where the river is known by rowers as the Gut, the Isis (as the Thames is called here) suddenly widens as the right bank swings round to the two footbridges at Longbridges. The boathouse next door belongs to Hertford College. Ahead can be seen more boathouses and the first Oxford spire - Christ Church. The towpath is alongside more meadows. Shortly on the far bank the River Cherwell joins the Thames on the two sides of the line of college boathouses. On the towpath is the Oxford University Boat Club.

RIVER CHERWELL entered the Thames only at the higher confluence until the new cut was made downstream in 1884. This new and now main channel was necessary because the river flows were opposed to each other. When the Cherwell was fast-flowing in 1663 the Thames was driven back a mile causing a tidal bore. On other occasions a fast-flowing Thames often drove back the Cherwell causing flooding.

OXFORD UNIVERSITY BOAT CLUB was founded in 1839 with this building opening in 1881. The club produces the crew for the annual Boat Race in London as well as organising rowing within the University including the Bumping Races at the end of May. The boathouses opposite date from the 1930s and succeeded the college barges which were moored there.

There is a view across the water to Christ Church Meadow before the path crosses a footbridge with a view (left) of water flowing under Grandpont House.

GRANDPONT HOUSE, where a braid of the Thames flows underneath, was built in 1785 for Oxford's Town Clerk Sir William Elias Taunton. Almost a century later it was the residence of Alderman Thomas Randall, a hatter and unpopular magistrate who attempted to restrict pub opening hours. It remains a private house.

Beyond Isis House the towpath bears round to the left to run up on to Oxford's Folly Bridge.

FOLLY BRIDGE, the southern entry to Oxford, was built in 1827. The name recalls a tower which stood on the previous structure and not the present Caudwell's Castle built in 1849. Folly Bridge Store on the north end was built in 1844 as the tollhouse but free passage has been allowed since 1850. Salter Brothers, established in 1858, still operate from here although its former boatyard, originally an 1830 warehouse for goods sent by river to and from London, is now The Head of the River pub. Lewis Carroll set out from here in July 1862 with Alice Liddell and her sisters on a rowing trip upstream during which he unfolded the tale which became *Alice's Adventures in Wonderland*.

Cross the road and go ahead over the footbridge crossing the stream which runs under Grandpont House. With the winding river the towpath runs under Salter's crane, in front of Jubilee Terrace, and under both a footbridge and a former railway bridge.

GAS BRIDGES The footbridge, open to the public since 1972, was completed in 1886 to carry pipes and pedestrians between gasworks on two sides of the river. The larger upstream bridge carried a railway branch line into sidings at the gasworks which closed in 1958. On the far bank, just beyond the railway bridge, water from the Oxford canal and upstream river flows into the Thames. The river used to divide into several streams as it passed through Oxford and this stream may have been the main channel.

Round another bend there is the main line railway bridge (1850; rebuilt 1898). Bear right across the footbridge spanning Bulstrake Stream where a monument records a drowning in 1889. The mill stream joins on the far bank. When the towpath crosses the weir stream to Osney Lock there is a view ahead, just behind the derelict red brick mill, of the remains of Osney Abbey.

Beyond the lock the towpath is over the weir and along the side of Osney Island where there is the The Watermans Arms and a line of riverside houses to reach Osney Bridge after crossing Osney Stream.

Refreshments

Abingdon: The Mill House on the bridge. Open all day.

Abingdon: Gallery Tea Room next to TIC at end of Bridge. Open 8.30am-5pm daily except Sun mornings.

Abingdon: Wells cheese shop in Stert Street serves lunch on

weekdays.

Sandford: The King's Arms.

Iffley Meadows: The Isis. On towpath. Open to 4pm weekends.

Oxford (Folly Bridge): The Head of the River pub. Open all day in summer.

Accommodation

Abingdon: 22 East St Helen Street, OX14 5EB (01235 533278).

Abingdon: 1 The Copse, OX14 3YW (01235 527158).

Abingdon: Barrows End, 3 The Copse, OX14 3YW (01235 523541).

Abingdon: Brewers Cottage, 3 Brewers Court, Winsmore Lane, OX14 5BG (01235 522324).

Transport

Abingdon: Rail (Thames Trains/Great Western/Virgin Trains) to Oxford then bus (Stagecoach Oxford 24hr service or Oxford Bus Company).

Oxford: Rail (Thames Trains/Great Western/Virgin Trains).

Tourist Information

Abingdon: 25 Bridge Street, OX14 3HN (01235 522711).

Map

OS Landranger 164 (Oxford).

The Rose Revived mooring

17. Oxford to Newbridge

13¹/₂ miles

This is the remotest stretch with a ferry to catch and poor public transport at the far end. Booking accommodation in advance is strongly advised. Other features include a treacle well, abbey ruins, the river's most northerly point, a toll bridge and miles of meadows. Those wishing to use the alternative but original towpath route involving the ferry at Bablock Hythe, rather than the official diversion from the river, may wish to phone ahead to check running times.

OXFORD, founded just before the Conquest on land where the Thames briefly divided into streams, is a University city with colleges dating from 1249. It is also home of Britain's oldest museum, The Ashmolean, which opened in 1683. Blackwell's, one of the world's largest bookshops, was established in 1879 - just five years after Frank Cooper launched his wife's Oxford Marmalade. Among the many who came upstream as students were Percy Shelley from

140

Eton in 1810 and Matthew Arnold from Laleham in 1841.

OSNEY BRIDGE, spelt and pronounced 'Oseney' until the 1920s, was maintained by Osney Abbey which was to the south on the left bank. A surviving 14th-century stone barn with a high roof can be seen from Osney Lock - the railway cuts through the Lady Chapel site. The Augustinian abbey, founded in 1129 just outside the city, had such impressive buildings at its dissolution in 1539 that Henry VIII briefly made it a cathedral. After four years that role was assumed by Christ Church and Osney's stones were eventually used for Civil War defences. The now main Thames channel, between the gasworks railway bridge and Port Meadow, was cut by the monks around 1227 to drive their mill. The present bridge, built in 1888 after the 18th-century structure collapsed sending a child to her death, has the lowest headroom on the river.

At Osney Bridge the towpath begins on the left bank. The channel, being probably manmade, is narrow giving a good view of allotments on the far side. At the bridge, crossing a link to the Old Thames at a point known as Tumbling Bay (a male only bathing area until 1892), continue ahead. There is water on both sides before the towpath passes on to Fiddler's Island. When the way is running between the New (left) and Old Thames do not cross the bridge to Port Meadow but continue ahead past Medley Boat Station. Cross the arched Rainbow Bridge (left) from where there is a view down on to the dividing river. On the right bank the towpath passes through Bossom's Boatyard.

BOSSOM'S BOATYARD The family includes generations of lock-keepers, weir-keepers and ferrymen. In 1880 Charlie Bossom towed William Morris upstream to Newbridge. The family connection here continued for another 90 years. This spot was once known as Medley Flash Lock which was just below the bridge.

Where the now wide track strikes away from the river towards nearby Binsey is the approximate location of a ford to Port Meadow.

BINSEY FORD may be the original ford of Ox-ford. Until early this century there was a ford here once used by pilgrims to St Margaret's Well at Binsey. St Frideswide's blindness was cured at the treacle (medicinal) well which later featured in *Alice's Adventures in Wonderland*. When restoration of the well was proposed Lewis Carroll advised "leave well alone".

PORT MEADOW The 342 acre grassland was given to Oxford as a common by William the Conqueror. The ground has never been ploughed or built on and rare plants flourishing include creeping marshwort and round fruited rush. Two hundred Oxford freemen and the commoners of Binsey and Wolvercote have grazing rights. The meadow's southern end floods in winter to occasionally become a popular skating rink.

Go ahead through the gate to stay by the river which bends west to pass The Perch.

THE PERCH The 17th-century thatched pub, which has log fires in winter, is said to be haunted by a sailor.

The next bend gives a view of Godstow Lock and the ruined Abbey.

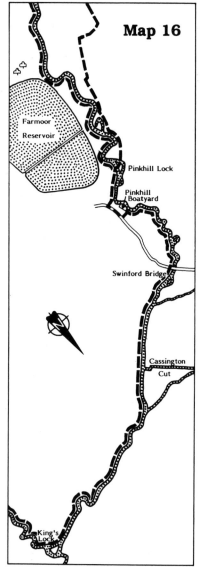

Map 16

142

GODSTOW means 'God's place'. The Abbey was founded in 1133 by Lady Edith Launceline who from Binsey saw a shaft of light touch the ground here. King Stephen was present at its consecration and it was a place of pilgrimage when the body of Rosamund de Clifford, Henry II's mistress poisoned by Queen Eleanor, was buried here - later the body was moved. The convent buildings became ruins in the Civil War but the Abbey hospice on the far bank continues to offer hospitality as The Trout Inn. Its garden always has peacocks and there is a view of Oxford's spires. Here on the bank Lewis Carroll's rowing party picnicked in 1862 having set out from Oxford.

Climb the bank ahead to a gate and cross the end of Godstow Bridge to continue on the towpath. Just beyond a Conservancy bridge there is an Oxford City boundary marker. Pass under the A34 road to the King's Lock access road which runs direct to the lock whilst the towpath follows two loops on the winding river. The footbridge carries the towpath over Wytham Stream which later rejoins the river as the Bulstake Stream.

Pass through King's Lock at the river's most northerly point. Soon there is a view ahead of Cassington Church spire. The river's double bend here is known as Hagley Pool. Beyond the footbridge many cut the corner but the towpath of course stays by the river. After a mile of farmland there is a view of the River Evenlode joining the Thames. A little further on it is possible to look across the river and straight down Cassington Cut.

CASSINGTON CUT is a canal dug to allow barges to pass easily up to Cassington Mill 1/2 mile inland on the last winding stretch of the River Evenlode which rises near Moreton-in-Marsh.

The towpath is now below Wytham Great Wood where deer occasionally come down to the river. After a second high kissing gate - to keep deer in - the way rises and passes through a TC gate by a stile. At a fork go right to cross a bridge and reach Eynsham Lock. Beyond is Swinford Bridge.

SWINFORD BRIDGE was probably designed by Sir William Taylor, friend of Blackstone who masterminded the 1767 Swinford Bridge Act. In 1765 the Earl of Abingdon bought the ferry (once run by nearby Eynsham Abbey) in order to replace it and a ford (John Wesley had ridden across the year before) with the elegant bridge completed in 1769. As the Earl paid for the bridge the Act allowed him and his successors to collect tolls tax free. Apart from a decimalization adjustment, Parliament has approved only one toll increase - since 1994 cars are 5p which is similar to the old 5d car charge based on five wheels including the spare one. Under the Act the ferry must be restored if the bridge falls down. The still privately owned bridge passed out of the Abingdon family in 1979.

Pass under the bridge and over a high stile. Here there is a tendency to cut a corner as the river bends - so much that it has created Horseshoe Island - to reach Oxford Cruiser Boatyard at Pinkhill.

PINKHILL BOATYARD There is a handy shop hidden on the riverfront at the side of a workshop. The boatyard has the last phone box for those wishing to check if Bablock Hythe Ferry is running - see Pinkhill Lock below and 'Pinkhill Towpath Route' at the end of this chapter.

Just beyond the boatyard the towpath is lost - unchecked erosion has long left a row of houses with gardens running down to the water. Due to the missing towpath it is necessary to make a detour up to the boatyard's vehicle entrance. Go right along the road past the houses. At the side of Pinkhill Lodge turn down a narrow path which leads back to the towpath at a footbridge. A firm path now runs to Pinkhill Lock where the Thames Path passes just outside the lock compound.

PINKHILL Lock, once Pinckle Lock, dates from 1791. Today the lock marks the start of a long Thames Path diversion from the towpath.

Choice of Route

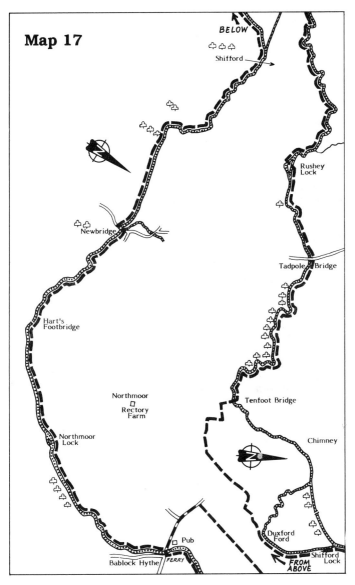

Map 17

BELOW

Shifford

Rushey
Lock

Newbridge

Tadpole Bridge

Hart's
Footbridge

Northmoor
Rectory
Farm

Tenfoot Bridge

Chimney

Northmoor
Lock

Duxford
Ford

Pub

Shifford
Lock

Bablock Hythe   FERRY

FROM
ABOVE

> ## *The Thames Path Official Route inland to Babcock Hythe*

In order not to rely on the ferry at Bablock Hythe the Thames Path crosses the lock and follows an inland route to Bablock Hythe. However, the towpath can be followed to Bablock Hythe and directions are given at the end of this chapter.

To continue on the Thames Path official route go right at the lock through a gate marked 'permitted path' and over the up-stream lock gates. Go forward and bear half left on to grass to go past a lamp post and through the trees to cross the weir.

On the far side there is a stile. Go half left across a large field to meet the river again beyond another stile. Keep by the river to go over a couple of stiles ahead. The far bank was part of an island. Here bear half right and soon the path runs alongside the old channel. The path joins the present navigation again at a point where the lost Skinner's Bridge crossed.

Look out for a lonely post which marks where the path veers away from the water - or rather keeps ahead as the river bends away. Walk to the far corner of the large field where there is a farm gate. Go through the gate and bear round to the right with the track to cross a stream. Now bear half left across to the far corner of this smaller field. In the corner there are two gates. Do not go through the wooden one - where in winter there may be a view of both the church tower and Pope's Tower at Stanton Harcourt - but through the waymarked gate to continue south.

Follow the hedge on the right which gives way to a gate and stile. Go over this stile on the right to follow a hedged road. Round the bend, at a junction, go through a narrow bridleway gate on the left. Continue south through six fields to reach a lane.

Turn left and at a junction continue forward past a caravan site to reach The Ferryman Inn at Bablock Hythe Ferry.

BABLOCK HYTHE FERRY, said to date from 950, is mentioned by Matthew Arnold in *The Scholar Gypsy* (1853): "Crossing the stripling Thames at Bablock-hithe." The ferry is operated by The Ferryman Inn previously called The Chequers and more recently The Ferry

Inn. A three vehicle ferry closed in 1965 to be replaced (after a brief 1981 revival) by the present 12 seat boat in 1992.

The Thames Path does not cross the river but continues right upstream through a series of gates and stiles by meadows. Just after TC gate 60 the river bends. Beyond the next bend the far bank is wooded as far as Northmoor Lock.

(Those staying at Northmoor's Rectory Farm should leave the river just before the stile in front of the overhead wires. Go along the field boundary and right at the north end for a few yards to a gate. Follow a wide path - known as The Causeway - over several fields to a road. Turn left for Rectory Farm next to the church.)

Despite the tread, the towpath does not cut the corner to the lock. After a mile there is Hart's Footbridge spanning the river. Pass the bridge to go over a stile and later there is a succession of three gates. After crossing a footbridge there is an official short cut across a corner to a TC gate. Enter a field to find the bridge at Newbridge flanked by two pubs. Ahead is The Rose Revived.

Refreshments

Oxford: St Aldate's Coffee House (opposite Christ Church). 11.30-2.30pm.

Oxford: Convocation Coffee House, University Church, High Street. 10am (11 Sun) -6pm (5pm Sun & winter).

Binsey: The Perch. Children welcome. 11.30am-3pm & 6.30-11pm; all day in summer (Sun 12-2.30pm & 7.-10.30pm).

Pinkhill: Shop at boatyard.

Bablock Hythe: The Ferryman. Two bars. Real ale. 11.30-3.30pm & 6.30-11.pm (Sun 12-3.30pm & 7-9.30pm; open all day summer weekends).

Accommodation

Oxford: Combermere House, 11 Polstead Rd, OX2 6TW (01865 556971).

Oxford: Falcon Hotel, 88-89 Abingdon Rd, OX1 4PX (01865 722995).

Oxford: 58 St John Street, OX1 2QR (01865 515454).

Oxford: The Falcon Private Hotel, 88-90 Abingdon Road, OX1 4PX.

Kings Lock: campsite (01865 553403).

Eynsham Lock: campsite.

Pinkhill Lock: campsite.

Bablock Hythe: The Ferryman, OX8 1BL (01865 880028). Also campsite.

Northmoor Lock: Field campsite (01865 862908). Mar-Oct.

Northmoor: Rectory Farm, OX8 4PX (01865 300207). Feb-Nov, Sun-Thu. 16th-century farmhouse, once belonging to St John's College Oxford. Picnic lunches if notice given.

Transport

Oxford: Rail (Thames Trains / Great Western / Virgin Trains).

Newbridge: Bus (Stagecoach 66) from Longworth to Oxford then rail (Thames Trains / Great Western / Virgin Trains).

Tourist Information

Oxford: The Old School, Gloucester Green, OX1 2DA (01865 726871).

Map

OS Landranger 164 (Oxford).

Pinkhill Lock Towpath Route

Here, where the Thames Path leaves the river to follow an alternative waymarked route to Bablock Hythe avoiding Bablock Hythe Ferry, the towpath continues to the ferry, operated by The Ferryman pub. The ferry runs most days except in bad weather or when there are strong winter currents. Walkers are advised to phone ahead to check running times on 01865 880028.

At Pinkhill Lock the towpath continues ahead by the river which bears left. After a stile at the bend the path enters Pinkhill Meadow. Take the right fork to stay on the towpath. To the left is a wetland created in 1990 as part of the nature reserve which is noted for its dragonflies. Soon after a lonely gauge station there

148

is a view down a backwater which was once the main channel. The paths converge at Farmoor Reservoir intake.

FARMOOR RESERVOIR INTAKE The huge reservoir was built on often flooded land in 1977 to supply water to much of Oxfordshire and as far as Swindon. Between the intake and the downstream backwater on the left bank there was a loop until 1899 when cutting the present short straight channel was completed.

Briefly the path is away from the water screened by trees before bending back at a gated bridge over a muddy backwater at a point still called Skinner's Bridge.

SKINNER'S BRIDGE crossed the Thames here on the line of Skinner's Weir which became dilapidated and collapsed in 1880. The replacement bridge was burnt down by Oxford undergraduates in the 1930s. The spot was originally called Langley Weir but became Skinner's after the family who for generations ran The Fish, a thatched pub, which was here until about 1876. The backwater bridge with a TC gate is on the line of lock gates at the entrance to a cut. The Fish was between the lock cut and the Thames so someone crossing the gates could continue along the side of the pub and over the weir to the left bank where there is still a three way path junction.

Once over the gated footbridge rejoin the riverbank. The trees over to the left indicate the line of the old lock cut. There is a slight dip as the towpath passes over the end of the former channel. On the far bank is a lonely post where the official Thames Path veers away from the river on its way to Bablock Hythe. Just beyond the end of the reservoir (left) there are a couple of TC gates before the path enters a long meadow. Soon there is a caravan site on the far bank. At the far end of the meadow a stile leads to Bablock Hythe Ferry where the towpath crosses the river. Hammer the bell on the tree to call the ferryboat; small charge.
Those who find themselves stuck on the right bank unable to reach the pub should turn inland on the road and take the bridlepath (left) to Cumnor where there are regular buses back to Oxford.

BABLOCK HYTHE See p146

Erosion at Shifford

18. Newbridge to Lechlade
17 miles

The Thames here is unspoilt but can also be lonely. As recently as the 1980s the towpath between Tenfoot Bridge and Tadpole was impenetrable. The approach to Lechlade is past William Morris's Kelmscott Manor where Compton Mackenzie wrote "on this stile Swinburne may have sat; there Burne-Jones may have looked back at the sky; and ...Rosetti tied up his shoe...". Booking accommodation ahead is again advised although at Lechlade there is more choice, and more buses than at Newbridge.

NEWBRIDGE, the second oldest bridge on the river, is 'new' because it was built after Radcot Bridge. Newbridge, with six pointed medieval arches and dating from around 1250, was built by Benedictines from St Denis near Paris who were living at nearby Northmoor. They placed the bridge in the care of a hermit whose tollhouse on the south side has become The Maybush. The builders used Taynton Quarry stone brought here on the River Windrush which joins on the north upstream side. Four hundred years later Wren had Taynton stone floated down to London for St Paul's Cathedral. Earlier this bridge had been the scene of two Civil War skirmishes. The Rose Revived on the north side until recently had a sign, painted in 1919 by Alfred Parsons RA, showing roses being revived with Morland's ale. It has also been called The Crown and The Fair House after fairs held here at Michaelmas.

Cross the bridge from The Rose Revived to turn down the side of The Maybush. Go through the TC gate. A causeway takes the towpath towards the river. After a kissing gate and a TC gate the path runs below a slope and through trees. Later there is a new Conservancy gate. At the river bend there is a gated footbridge leading to a meadow. The first few yards of the path are along a still discernible island known as Haul Ham.

Stay by the river round several bends and then through a copse of pollarded willows. One towpath bridge is beginning to become isolated by erosion. After a gated TC bridge, opposite Shifford Church on the far bank, the Great Brook entry can be seen.

SHIFFORD King Alfred is said to have held the first meeting of an English 'parliament' here in 890. The community has declined, leaving a farm and the once Georgian church rebuilt in 1863. There was a flash lock here before Shifford Lock was built upstream. The Great Brook was dug in the mid-19th century as an irrigation channel stretching back $2^{1}/2$ miles towards Bampton.

The path continues alongside a field and before the end there is a view of Shifford Lock. A bridge leads to Shifford Island.

SHIFFORD LOCK CUT opened in 1897 after a year's work which created an island. The idea was not just to avoid a $1^{1}/4$ mile loop and save $^{3}/4$ mile but to remove a twisting and shallow navigation which was forcing barge traffic to turn back at Newbridge. Chimney-on-Thames, the farm north of the cut, belonged to the Church Commissioners until 1921 but continued to be farmed by the Gauntlett family, who had arrived at the end of the 19th century, until 1994. The footbridge crossing, replacing a lost ferry across the Old Thames to the lock, opened in 1994 as part of the proposed Thames Path route. However, although it is possible to cross on to

Shifford Island and explore the lock cut, the Thames Path is at present along the old towpath by the Old Thames.

Pass the footbridge (right) to reach the field corner where the towpath continues between two TC posts. The way is very narrow and was overgrown in the 1980s. Along the way there is a TC gate, some steps and a small plank bridge. Further on the path runs between TC gateposts and eventually high above the river before descending at steps to the ford at Duxford.

DUXFORD At this ford the old towpath switched to the left bank. The old upstream stretch of towpath no longer exists but it is possible to cross to a public footpath which runs across the island to the cut. However, walkers are warned that crossing the ford can be dangerous - especially when the river is running high in winter. Duxford Farm, immediately upstream on the right bank, is part of the St Thomas' Hospital estate.

The path continues away from the river and past a cottage. At a road turn right and follow the metalled surface to Duxford Farm. Do not turn right into the farmyard but continue ahead on the rough track over a bridge. At once go right and left to follow a hedge (left). At the far end continue into the next field. The path runs ahead across the middle passing a lonely tree to the left. Also over to the left are a couple of derelict buildings. The official path cuts the corner so at the far end go right for a few yards to look for an entry leading to a footbridge. From the bridge there is a view half left up to Buckland where the church dominates the village. Go right along the edge of the field and through the gap at the end to cross a bridge. Turn left to follow a ditch (left) and after a short distance turn right down a high hedged way to find Tenfoot Bridge at the end.

TENFOOT BRIDGE dates from 1869 when the bridge replaced a weir which had a 10ft gap for navigation.

Cross the bridge to rejoin the towpath and turn left. The river winds and the towpath tends to be narrow and slightly overgrown. Progress can seem slow here. There is an occasional TC gate or a stile - often set back from the riverside. After a second pronounced bend the way is suddenly fairly clear as it runs along the top of a flood bank. Ahead can be seen Tadpole Bridge.

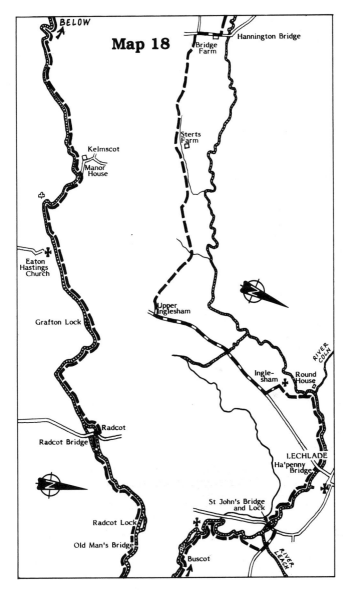

BELOW

Map 18

Hannington Bridge

Bridge
Farm

Sterts
Farm

Kelmscot

Manor
House

Eaton
Hastings
Church

Grafton Lock

Upper
Inglesham

RIVER COLN

Ingle-
sham

Round
House

Radcot

Radcot Bridge

LECHLADE
Ha'penny
Bridge

St John's Bridge
and Lock

Radcot Lock

Old Man's Bridge

Buscot

RIVER LEACH

TADPOLE BRIDGE was probably built in 1789 with a toll gate between the bridge and The Trout on the right bank. The 17th-century inn is the only building here. The first mention of the name is on a 1761 map where the spelling is 'Tadpoll'. From 1791 until 1914 there was a wharf here for Bampton $1^{1}/_{2}$ miles to the north. The toll gate lasted until 1875.

The towpath continues ahead on a metalled road which runs for a mile to Rushey Lock. Go through the gate to cross the lower gates and pass the hut and cottage. Cross the weir and at once turn right to a TC gate. The towpath is now by meadows and briefly under old willows. There are tempting short cuts where the river bends but one can lose the water.

From Old Man's Bridge the way is metalled as far as nearby Radcot Lock. A long grass path leads to a TC gate and at the end of the next meadow there is an unusual double gate. After a bend Radcot Bridge comes into view. Go over Cradle Bridge (crossing the old river course) and stay on the right path by the main navigation to reach Radcot. The Swan is on the far bank.

RADCOT There has been a bridge here since 958. The Earl of Oxford had leapt over a gap here on his horse when fleeing from battle in 1387 so the present medieval bridge probably dates from 1393 with work undertaken by Normandy monks who lived at Faringdon. The downstream parapet has a niche for a Virgin Mary statue. May Morris (daughter of William) added the statue to her sketch of the river's oldest bridge which she saved from falling into dangerous disrepair with a vigorous campaign just before the First World War. Navigation is under a new bridge built in 1787 when a backstream was enlarged to cope with traffic using the Thames & Severn Canal. Radcot House to the north is 17th century. The farmland on the left downstream bank belongs to the moated Friars Court Farm on the site of a Knights Hospitaller preceptory.

Cross the navigation channel to the left bank to find the tow-path continuing beyond a TC gate. The river runs south-west and north-west to curve round to Grafton Lock. After a riverside pillbox there is a double stile and an early view of Eaton Hastings Church on the far bank. This is later seen beyond a fine lawn.

EATON HASTINGS Church is partly Norman. 'Hastings' comes from

Ralph de Hastings who owned the village in the 12th century. Eaton Hastings House alongside was home of the *Mirror* executive Lord Ryder of Eaton Hastings until 1984.

There is a brief view half right of Lechlade Church spire. On crossing a stile by a pillbox it is possible to see (half right) the chimneys of Kelmscott Manor. After a double bend there is a stile and gate where the towpath becomes a track. Across to the left is a view of Buscot Park's mansion. At the Kelmscot mooring a track leads off to the right into the village.

KELMSCOT Artist and manufacturer William Morris, who first saw the village from the river approach, lived at Kelmscott Manor from 1871 until his death in 1896 at Hammersmith. He described this house as "heaven on earth" and walked the riverbank collecting reeds, grasses and flowers for dyes and patterns for textiles. When the meadows flooded the post was delivered by punt and the Morris family would cross the grass in a flat bottomed boat. His utopian story *News From Nowhere* ends with travellers arriving at Kelmscot. Morris is buried in the churchyard of the partly Norman church which he helped to 'preserve' rather than 'restore'. The spirit of Morris lives on with even the village hall designed by Morris disciple Ernest Gimson and opened by Bernard Shaw. The Manor, in the hands of the Society of Antiquaries, is open on the first Wed, Apr-Sep; 11am-5pm; admission charge.

Cross the gated footbridge into a field to follow the towpath to a wood by Eaton Footbridge crossing.

EATON FOOTBRIDGE There was a flash lock here known as Hart's Weir after a family who supplied the lock-keepers for generations. The Anchor Inn, on the right bank, was burnt down in 1979.

Keep past the bridge. A TC gate leads into a field and Gloucestershire is reached at a stile. Afterwards the path is clear as the river enjoys several bends. Opposite the most southerly point is the former entrance to a short canal which led to a brick and tile works at inland Buscot Wharf. Later the towpath crosses a footbridge on to an island to reach Buscot Lock.

BUSCOT village has a well, hall and houses built by the 1st Lord Faringdon of the nearby 18th-century Buscot Park. In the mid-20th

155

century the 2nd Lord Faringdon hosted Fabian Society gatherings there and added Labour heritage murals. The riverside Cotswold stone Old Parsonage was built in 1703 alongside the church which has a 15th-century tower and two Burne-Jones windows. The large 'island' upstream of the lock on the Buscot side was known as Brandy Island when in 1859 Robert Campbell, who preceeded Lord Faringdon at Buscot Park, set up the Berkshire Distillery on the island and exported the alcohol to France by river via London. A tramway ran to Buscot Wharf downstream. A little upstream of the Parsonage is a spot called Cheese Wharf where Gloucester cheeses were landed from small craft to be loaded into barges for London.

The towpath continues, not across the lock gates, but over the bridge. Do not go over the TC stile but left along the edge of the huge meadow. At a bend there is a fine view of Buscot Church and the Old Parsonage with two busts on the wall. There are three bends, with views of Lechlade spire, before the path reaches Bloomer's Hole where the path switches banks.

BLOOMER'S HOLE Unfortunately well advanced plans announced in 1993 for a single span bridge with clear glass balustrades on the line of the old ferry have been abandoned following local objections. A bridge should be erected in late 1999. It has been suggested that at this spot there was a flash lock for holding deep water for upstream moorings. The origin of the name is obscure although 'hole' means 'place where water is deep'.

Walk up the long straight path running inland. Turn left along the road, crossing the tiny River Leach and passing a caravan park, to a junction. Go left to pass The Trout and cross (with care) St John's Bridge back into Oxfordshire (Berkshire until 1974). On the far side a stepped path runs down from a gate to St John's Lock.

ST JOHN'S BRIDGE & LOCK A series of wooden bridges here was replaced by a stone crossing in 1229 and soon after the Priory of St John was built on the left bank with the monks maintaining the bridge. The Trout, formerly The St John the Baptist's Head, was opened as a pub by the monks in 1472. Three years later Edward IV dissolved the seven strong community but left one priest in charge of the bridge. The pub has inherited the Priory's fishing rights. During the Civil War General Fairfax rode over from the south with troops ready to rout the

Lechlade Royalists. The present bridge was erected in 1886. The lock, opened in 1790 and rebuilt in 1905, is the last and highest on the river. In 1830 the lock-keeper was also running The Trout. The lock's Old Father Thames, made for the 1851 Great Exhibition, stood at the Source from 1958 to 1974.

Go through the gate at the end of the lock compound and after a short distance cross a footbridge (which spanned a now diverted spur of the River Cole) marking the boundary between Oxfordshire (Old Berkshire) and Wiltshire. After a short distance there is a gate next to the last TC stile. Stay by the winding river with the Lechlade spire always in view. On approaching Lechlade's Halfpenny

*Old Father Thames
at St John's Lock*

Bridge there is a clear view across to the sweeping lawns and archway of The New Inn in Lechlade. Go through the gates on each side of the towpath tunnel under Halfpenny Bridge. Steps on the left lead up onto the bridge and the road running into Lechlade.

Refreshments

Newbridge: The Rose Revived. Soup, ploughman's and vegetarian dishes. Open 11am-11pm. (Sun 12-10.30pm.)

Tadpole: The Trout Inn. Real ale, bar snacks. Children welcome. Open 11am-11pm in summer. Closed 3-5.30pm winter weekdays. (Sun 12-10.30pm.)

Radcot: The Swan. By the river. Children welcome. Log fire in winter.

Kelmscot: The Plough. Children welcome. Open all day.

St John's Bridge: The Trout. Soup, local sausages & vegetarian dishes. Children welcome. Open 11am-3pm (food 12-2pm); 6-11pm (food 7-10pm) & all day summer Sats. (Sun 12-3pm & 7-10.30pm)

Accommodation

Newbridge: The Rose Revived (01865 300221).

Tadpole: The Trout Inn campsite, Tadpole Bridge, SN7 8RD (01367 870382)

Shifford Lock: Chimney House, Chimney-on-Thames OX18 2EH (01367 870279). Mar-Nov. Cross footbridge to Shifford Island, pass lock to follow cut and cross bridge to follow road to Chimney.

Bampton: Romany Inn, Bridge Street, OX18 2HA (01993 850162).

Bampton (2 mile footpath walk north from Rushey Lock): Morar, Weald Street, OX18 2HL (01993 850162). Non-smoking farmhouse.

Kelmscot: The Plough, GL7 3HG (01367 253543).

Kelmscot: Manor Farm (01367 52620). 2 family double rooms in NT owned farmhouse. Evening meals available.

Buscot: Apple Tree House, SN7 8DA (01367 252592).

St John's Bridge: St John's Priory Park campsite, GL7 3EH (01367 252360). Mar-Oct.

Transport

Newbridge: Rail (Thames Trains/Great Western/Virgin Trains) to Oxford then bus (Stagecoach 66) to Longworth then walk.

Lechlade: Bus (Thamesdown/Stagecoach 77) to Swindon then rail (Great Western/Thames Thames).

Maps

OS Landranger 164 (Oxford) and 163 (Cheltenham).

Halfpenny Bridge at Lechlade

19. Lechlade to Cricklade

10¹⁄₄ miles

Soon after Lechlade the towpath ends and, although navigation is technically allowed as far as Cricklade, only canoes now make it any further upstream as the river is narrow and shallow. In the 1850s it was often full of tall reeds but was cleared by the 1870s which allowed for about 3ft of water for some navigation. For today's walkers there are two long diversions on main roads until new riverside paths, 'extending' the towpath, are created.

LECHLADE is mentioned in Domesday Book. Its landmark church has been described as one of the six best in Gloucestershire. The perfect perpendicular building dates from 1476 and may have been dedicated to St Lawrence at the wish of Catherine of Aragon who later held the manor. Her pomegranate symbol can be found on the vestry door. The rare Chapel of St Blaise, patron of woolcombers, has combs painted on the reredos and recalls the wool sent to London by river. Even before the Thames & Severn Canal opened

Lechlade was a busy port for London. The very early 18th-century Church House in the churchyard was built by John Aing who ran a wharf behind for landing London goods. The garden has a fine gazebo seen from Shelley Walk which recalls the poet's visit in 1815 when he stayed two nights at The New Inn and wrote *A Summer-evening Churchyard, Lechlade*. Later Compton Mackenzie featured the town as 'Ladingford' in his novel *Guy and Pauline*, writing "the spire of the church remained so long in sight".

HALFPENNY BRIDGE Until this bridge was completed in 1793 most traffic had to use St John's Bridge as only pedestrians could use a ferry at the end of Bell Lane. This bridge was made high to avoid the need to lower masts on all the new barges passing under from the new Thames & Severn Canal. The arched stones are arranged radially as with the first Westminster Bridge which had just been built. The tollhouse remains although the bridge has been toll free since 1875. The ¹/₂d toll which gave the crossing its name was levied on walkers (except churchgoers and mourners) until 1839.

Steps lead down on the south upstream side to the towpath. Continue upstream and from the meadow side path there is a view over to the last boatyard on the river. The last TC gate used to be here between Lechlade and Inglesham. Cross a footbridge (over a braid) to leave Wiltshire and enter Gloucestershire for a short period. Soon there is the last bridge over the navigable Thames. A few yards further on is the footing of the now lost footbridge which carried the towpath over the river to continue along the canal which began by the Round House opposite.

THE ROUND HOUSE marks the end of navigation on the Thames which flows to the left of the building. To the right is the former entrance to the Thames & Severn Canal which from 1789 took navigation on beyond the source to join the Stroudwater Navigation. Suddenly salt from Droitwich and fruit from Evesham came down the Thames to London. Percy and Mary Shelley, Charles Clairmont and Thomas Love Peacock arrived here in a rowing boat in September 1815 intending to go up the canal but found the £20 toll too steep. Instead they continued on the river towards Inglesham Church but when the reeds became too thick and the water too shallow they stopped rowing and allowed the flow to carry them back towards Halfpenny Bridge. Canal traffic was eventually reduced by the arrival of the railways which even reached Lechlade. The waterway was abandoned in 1933 but now the Stroudwater & Severn Canal Trust is engaged on a long restoration programme.

Continue by the Thames as it double bends to Murdock Ditch (once a significant braid), on the Gloucestershire-Wiltshire boundary. Cross a footbridge (which is now a little inland) to re-enter Wiltshire. From here head across a field towards the left side of the buildings at Inglesham. A stile leads to a road. The church is to the right just beyond Inglesham House.

INGLESHAM is the site of a lost village where only a 13th-century church and a farm remain. The redundant church on a mound was saved from over restoration in the 19th century by William Morris who loved its old simplicity and box pews. There are wall paintings and a Virgin and Child carving on the south wall.

There is no riverside path so the Thames Path continues to the left from the stile to reach a T-junction at the main road. Go right along the main road for just over a mile, crossing the River Cole, to Upper Inglesham. (The verge on the left may prove better than being on the right facing on-coming traffic.)
At Upper Inglesham go right to pass Middle Hill Farm on the corner and the Forge Restaurant. At the bend go through a gate on the right on to a bridleway. The path runs straight ahead alongside a large field. There are several gates on the way linked sometimes to temporary fencing. A final view (right) of Lechlade Church is possible just before the path bears round to the left to ford a stream. (There is a footbridge to the right.) Go through the gate and along the edge of a field. Where the hedge ends there can be seen a footbridge on the right which will one day bring the Thames Path on to this bridleway as it runs north from the river.
Continue ahead across open fields. Over to the left can be seen Highworth Church. The path veers to the left on drawing level with the abandoned Sterts Farm. After ³/₄ mile there is a gate and the way bears round to the right to meet a metalled road by a cottage. Turn left to a junction.
Ahead is Hannington Wick but the Thames Path continues to the right towards Hannington Bridge. There is a view half left of Kempsford Church. After Bridge Farm there is Hannington Bridge.

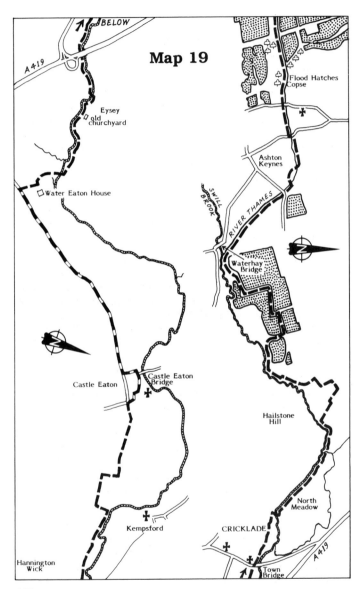

Map 19

BELOW

A 419

Eysey
old churchyard

☐ Water Eaton House

Flood Hatches
Copse

✝

Ashton
Keynes

SWILL BROOK

RIVER THAMES

Waterhay
Bridge

Castle Eaton
Bridge

Castle Eaton

✝

Hailstone
Hill

North
Meadow

Kempsford

✝

CRICKLADE

✝

Hannington
Wick

A 419

Town
Bridge

HANNINGTON BRIDGE, built in the early 1840s on the line of a Roman crossing, spans a (sometimes dry) braid of the Thames as well as the main channel with its left bank in Oxfordshire.

The walk continues on the Wiltshire bank across the road from Bridge Farm - there is a stile at the side of the gateway. Walk along the side of three fields linked by stiles, with the river braid to the right. At the corner of the third field there is a stile and footbridge. Continue alongside the river braid, passing a ford, to another footbridge at a point where the two channels meet. There are now the best views of Kempsford's church tower.

KEMPSFORD was a detached part of the Duchy of Lancaster. The landmark church tower was built in 1390 by John of Gaunt Duke of Lancaster in memory of his wife who had died in 1369. Behind the village is Fairfield airbase used by the US Air Force for many years including wartime and for testing Concorde.

At the field corner bear left with the hedge and at a gap turn right to find Blackford Farm at the start of Blackford Lane. Follow the road round two bends to reach Castle Eaton. Turn right to bear left into School Lane and go right up Long Row to the start of The Street. Opposite is the lychgate entrance to a long path up to the church. Continue along The Street to reach The Red Lion and the bridge.

CASTLE EATON The site of the castle is unknown but near the church there was a manor house which was turned into a fortress in 1311. The riverside church has Norman doorways and above its 13th-century chancel is a bell turret with the original 13th-century sanctus bell found and rehung in 1900. The present bell turret was added by William Butterfield when he undertook restoration in 1861 having just completed his work on the new St Alban's Holborn. In the nearby riverside Red Lion, a Georgian inn, there is a picture of the earlier bridge here which has been replaced by the iron structure.

Do not cross Castle Eaton Bridge but continue along The Street to a bend. Do not be tempted down Mill Lane ahead but go left to reach the main road. Until a riverside path is created it is necessary to follow a road route to Water Eaton. Go right and follow this road for 2 miles, with occasional views of Cricklade

church tower. (There may be a temporary way to the river waymarked on the right shortly after Plague Cottages. Until this is opened stay on the road to Water Eaton.) Although the main farm entrance at Water Eaton is a public right of way continue ahead for a short distance to find, just before Middle Farm Cottages, a permissive path on the right. Walk past two fields to go left and right at a pond. Ahead is a footbridge spanning the Thames.

Cross the footbridge and turn left upstream with the path. The path is briefly away from the winding bank as the River Ray joins on the far side. There are several bends but as the path appears to be running ahead towards Lechlade Church bear left to a stile to stay by the river. A long field slopes down to the river. Up on the hill is a wooded enclosure hiding Eysey churchyard - the early Victorian church, which replaced a medieval one once visible from the river, was pulled down in the 1953. The path curves in a half circle with the river before crossing to the other bank at a footbridge. Soon Down Ampney Brook flows into the Thames from the north side - there was a ford here in the last century.

After two stiles, and beyond a pipe bridge, there is a footbridge over a ditch - this was the mouth of the tiny River Key until the by-pass was built in 1975. Go under the new road and after a short distance go right over a farm bridge spanning the diverted River Key. Walk ahead towards Cricklade with the Thames on the right. Cross the stone stile at the farm buildings and bear over to the right to cross another stile leading to a lane. To the right is the ancient Hatchetts ford. But the Thames Path runs to the left up Thames Lane and right into Abingdon Court Lane to reach Cricklade High Street.

Refreshments

Lechlade: The Riverside, all day café and pub, next to Halfpenny Bridge.

Lechlade: The Bag of Flour in Burford Street. A fine bakery with picnic food.

Lechlade: The Café Upstairs above the Oxford Wine Company on the corner of Burford and St John Streets.

Lechlade: The Black Cat Restaurant & Tea Rooms, High Street. Open daily except Mon to 5pm.

Castle Eaton: The Red Lion, The Street. Food available 12-2pm and 7-9pm (not Wed evenings). Riverside garden.

Accommodation

Lechlade: Cambrai Lodge Guest House, Oak St, GL7 3AH (0144367 253173).

Lechlade: The New Inn, Market Square, GL7 3AB (01367 252296).

Lechlade: The Flour Bag (bakery), Burford Street, GL7 3AP (01367 252322).

Castle Eaton: The Red Lion, The Street (01285 810280).

Hannington Wick: The Manor (01285 8130009). Dinner available.

Transport

Lechlade: Rail (Great Western/Thames Trains) to Swindon then

bus (Thamesdown/ Stagecoach 77).

Cricklade:

Bus (Stagecoach 51) to Swindon then Rail (Great Western/ Thames Trains).

Map

OS Landranger 163 (Cheltenham).

Weir paddles

20. Cricklade to Source

12¼ miles

In the early 20th century there were people who could remember the Thames being open for barges as far as Waterhay Bridge due to the riverbed having being dragged by horses in a dry summer. This final section involves a diversion around lakes in the Cotswold Water Park before Waterhay is reached. Here the river changes dramatically in size and scenery for the final few miles. The Source is a lonely spot but there is both an unusual pub and a handy station nearby.

CRICKLADE means 'place by the river crossing' and the town motto, 'In Lovely Surroundings', is derived from a 12th-century document. Cricklade lies on a kink of the Roman built Ermin Street and has been described as an example of a Saxon new town. The landmark tower on St Sampson's Church was added by Lady Jane Grey's father-in-law just before his execution. Inside the tower is the Westminster Abbey shield (it held the church in Norman times) and mysteriously the spade, heart, diamond and club of the playing card which led William Morris to suggest that the tower was paid for by a successful gamble. Near Town Bridge is the older St Mary's which has a Norman chancel arch and since 1983 is again a Roman Catholic Church making it 'Britain's oldest Roman Catholic church'. In 1821 William Cobbett described Cricklade as a "villainous hole" due to its poverty. Then the Bath Road at the side of The Vale was the main road making the junction a crossroads. The market cross had already been moved to the churchyard but now the 1897 Jubilee Clock is the focal point at the junction. The wide main street sloping down to the Thames had a monthly cattle market until 1944. The White Hart, dating from at least James I's reign, was rebuilt in 1890. Nearby Michael Hart, a butcher's since the last century, is noted for its award winning sausages made to secret recipes handed down from his father who was a New Forest butcher. The ancient Hatchetts ford at the end of Thames Lane was the scene of Baptist baptisms into the early 20th century - in the Victorian era there was also the wooden Plank Bridge on the downstream side.

TOWN BRIDGE The first was built by the Romans who created the long causeway from the town crossing not only the Thames but also the River Churn and the water meadows. From above this bridge the river ceases to be open to craft. From Roman times until the 1830s there was a wharf on the east side of the road stretching south to just beyond the present war memorial. The bridge was rebuilt in 1854 to include, in the corner of the bus stop waiting area, steps (now gone) down to a 'watergate' where water could be drawn - an iron fence below protected children from falling into the river. Riverside, to the north, is the site of a tanyard and next door St John's Priory gave shelter and food to passersby from at least 1231 until the 1530s. The outline of the chapel window can be seen from the road.

At the north end of the High Street do not cross Town Bridge but go left along North Wall. Walk on the right near the Thames to leave the road after a short distance and go over a stile by a gate into a field. Keep forward and as the river swings away go over another stile into a large meadow. Continue forward near the left hand side of the meadow to find ahead a gap under a tree on the far side. Go ahead with houses to the left to reach the end of Bailiff's Piece (left). Ahead is number 4. Go through the kissing gate to the right.

Bear half left across the grass. The way narrows to a kissing gate and at a huge willow bears right over a railway sleeper footbridge to another kissing gate. Turn right and left round a shed on the site of West Mill to cross the river on a wide concrete bridge.

WEST MILL stood here from at least 1300 until demolished by Thames Conservancy in 1938. The rebuilt weir is a National Rivers Authority gauging weir measuring the quantity of water coming down. The mill took over the work of Town Mill which for a time was a few yards upstream from Town Bridge.

Once across the water turn left and follow the river. At the third stile the riverside path is alongside North Meadow.

NORTH MEADOW Centuries of regular hay cutting and grazing have caused this field filled with colourful flowers to become one of the finest uncultivated ancient meadows in Britain. Plants found include adder's tongue, great burnet, marsh marigold, water crowfoot, buttercups, celandines and the largest number anywhere of the rare snake's head fritillaries which flower in late April. Most of the fritillaries are purple although in the last thirty years there has been an increase in the number of white flowers. Once all the flowers were picked for local use or sent to Covent Garden but now picking is forbidden and visitors must keep to the public footpaths. Cutting of the organic hay begins on 1 July and, although most of the land is now owned by English Nature, different people - some using scythes - cut the old allotment areas as marked by the stones. On 12 August (Lammas Day in the Old Calendar) the Hayward (appointed by the Cricklade Court Leet) unpadlocks the gate to allow cattle to graze - until recently they were herded down Cricklade's main street and along the causeway. Horses go on in September and sheep take over in winter and, unless there is flooding from the Thames, stay until 12 February (Candlemas Eve in the Old Calendar).

Shortly before approaching the old canal crossing there is, by the water, one of the meadow allotment stones. Steps lead up to a stile on the bridge.

OLD CANAL BRIDGE, now rebuilt for a bridleway, was once a canal bridge taking the Latton-Swindon Canal, built in 1819 as a branch of the Thames & Severn Canal, across the Thames. The bed of the canal can be seen running north.

Do not cross the Thames but go through the gate (right) to continue down a slope and along the winding bank with the water to the left. There is a view back to the Cricklade church tower before the end of the field. Go over the stile to join a track as the Thames bears left curving south round Hailstone Hill to a former railway bridge.

HAILSTONE HILL, once Holy Stone Hill, had a chapel dedicated to St Helen. The hill was cut through by the Swindon-Cirencester railway line which opened in 1883. The track was lifted in 1964 and now forms a short section of the Thames Path.

Do not go over the stile under the bridge but follow the track up to the farm gate where there is a another stile. (Walkers are allowed to stay by the river for a short distance but the bank upstream of the bridge is not part of the Thames Path.) Once on the former railway embankment go right through a gate and walk ahead on the wide straight path which is part of the Cotswold Water Park.

COTSWOLD WATER PARK Extensive quarrying for sand and gravel through the 20th century has left numerous flooded pits which make up the 14,000 acre water park now offering sailing, windsurfing, fishing and even a beach experience for paddling. Several lakes are given over to wildlife. (Information: 01285 861459.) Unfortunately the gravel excavation has led to increased evaporation of exposed water and considerable changes in drainage patterns which has reduced the river's water flow between Ashton Keynes and Kemble.

Stay on the straight path for ¼ mile to a signpost pointing left to 'Ashton Keynes 3 miles'. Go left down the slope on the gravel path which bears right and bends twice more before reaching the second turning on the right. Go right (over steps to discourage motor-cyclists) and stay on this path which soon crosses a footbridge and bears left and right to run near the Thames.

After some distance there is a view of the Thames (left) passing under an old bridge. Here the gravel track divides. The left hand gate is marked 'No access' so take the right fork which runs north and then west (left) to a gate and along the top of Manor Brook Lake. The lakeside path bends three times before reaching a gate. Follow the enclosed path which passes two more lakes (right). As the path bends the Thames can just be seen over to the left. At a junction go left for a short distance to find a stile set back on the right.

However, it is rewarding to continue ahead to cross the sud-denly narrow Thames at the pedestrian entrance to Waterhay car park. To reach Waterhay Bridge go ahead to the road and turn left.

WATERHAY BRIDGE The water flowing under the bridge is the Swill Brook which becomes the Thames where the infant Thames joins from the north bank - a confluence which appears as a drainage ditch meeting a river. The imbalance is largely due to changes in the water table but the Swill Brook has already been fed by streams from the upstream Thames before reaching Waterhay. The bridge takes its name from a village to the south which has largely disappeared. So reduced was the population by 1896 that all but the 13th-century chancel of All Saints Church was moved to nearby Leigh and rededicated as St Leonard's. An annual service is held on All Saints Day at the redundant All Saints (which can be seen to the south-west from the bridge in winter). To visit the church go down the turning signposted 'Leigh' to pass Waterhay Farm and Chancel View (where the key can be borrowed) and go right across the field.

The Thames Path continues at the stile on the path from the car park.

The infant Thames is to the left. This area, still fields in the 1980s, was ruined in the early 1990s when gravel extraction tore out

the hedges and obliterated the Thames which ceased to enjoy a continuous flow along its historic channel. After ½ mile there is an old Thames bridge (left) which until 1995 was a public footpath. Just beyond here the riverbed (probably dry) is behind a hedge (left) as the Thames Path goes ahead through three kissing gates to a playing field. Walk in front of the pavilion to another kissing gate at the driveway. A short path ahead leads to the road at Rixon End on the edge of Ashton Keynes.

ASHTON KEYNES was described by William Cobbett in 1826 as "a very curious place". Many of the houses have bridges to cross the infant Thames. The village has four crosses (all damaged by Roundheads) and their origin is still a mystery. The one in the churchyard became the war memorial in 1917. The church, dating from Saxon times and appropriately dedicated to the Holy Cross, was restored in 1876-7 by Butterfield who enlarged the Norman chancel arch. Nextdoor Church Farm has a house with a moat fed by the Thames. Keynes is derived from the de Kaines family who arrived with William the Conqueror and became local landowners.

Go left for a few yards and then right down a waymarked path. Soon there is Bourne Cottage to the left. When the path turns sharp left to a stone footbridge do not cross the river but go right through a kissing gate into a field. Walk ahead with the river to the left to another kissing gate at the far end. Go left over the Thames and follow a lane with the Thames to the right.

At the T-junction, where the Thames disappears down the side of Bridge Cottage (ahead), the Thames Path turns right to follow Back Street. (To reach the village Post Office and shop go left and right into Fore Street.) In Back Street, which runs along the back of the village, there is The Plough Inn.

At the end of the road turn left into High Road to cross Gumstool Bridge over the Thames which flows from the side of a thatched cottage. Turn right by the cross to go up Church Walk alongside the now wider river. (Only cross the next bridge and continue on the opposite bank to visit Ashton Keynes Church.) The Thames Path is ahead where the river emerges from a narrow mill race. Beyond the corn mill passage the path is beside a field and the river begins to take on the nature of a canal. Some distance after a gate there is a view of Church Farm's moat entry.

Cross the road and continue ahead with a lake to the left and the

17th-century Manor House across the Thames. The path crosses a weir which sends water down to Swill Brook by way of a wood known as Flood Hatches Copse. The river does a gentle double bend before passing a track crossing and a footbridge. At the Wiltshire-Gloucestershire boundary, at the end of Freeth's Wood, the path is a little back from the river which is screened by growth. On the left there is another vast lake. Keep past a bridge with Lower Mill Lake to the left. The path switches bank at a footbridge - a ford until recently. Soon the Thames divides for Lower Mill Farm.

LOWER MILL FARM The mill was grinding cattle feed for local farms until the 1960s and the machinery remains intact.

The track is now metalled and the river is briefly lost. At the main road go ahead to the right end of the fence to find a lane running into Somerford Keynes.

SOMERFORD KEYNES Somerford means a place where the river can be crossed in summer and Keynes refers to the family of nearby downstream Ashton Keynes. The church, founded in 685 on land given by the King of Mercia to St Aldhelm, has a Saxon doorway on the south side. The nextdoor Manor House, shored up with buttresses when a floor was added in the 17th century, has a dovecot.

The Path used to go into the edge of the village and left for Neigh Bridge. Now the official Path route is left along the main road and right to reach Neigh Bridge.

Go ahead (not over the bridge) to follow the winding Thames riverbank on the edge of Neigh Bridge Country Park. To the right there is the last of the many lakes. At the end of the lake cross the Thames on a footbridge and stay on the left near the water. After a gate the path passes the partly 16th-century Kemble Mill - where a footpath crosses from the stile (left) to Somerford Keynes (right).

The Path continues past the stile (left) and along the hedge (masking the river) to a stile. Keep forward by the water crossing a bridge set back at an inlet. Here there is a first view of Somerford Keynes Church and Manor House (right). Go over a stile to pass Old Mill Farm. The Path, indicated by a couple of waymark posts, is away from the riverbank before swinging left back to the water after the farm. Keep by the fence (left) and do not be tempted over the footbridge. Later the Path crosses a footbridge over a stream feeding the Thames (left) to enter a field which has a windpump in the

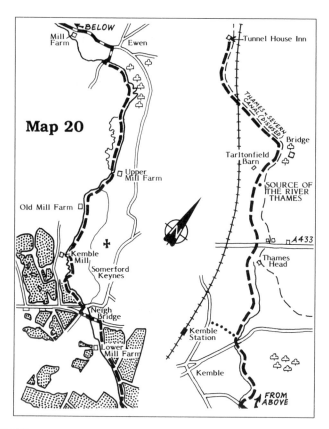

Map 20

Mill Farm
BELOW
Ewen
Upper Mill Farm
Old Mill Farm
Kemble Mill
Somerford Keynes
Neigh Bridge
Lower Mill Farm

Tunnel House Inn
THAMES & SEVERN CANAL (DISUSED)
Bridge
Tarltonfield Barn
SOURCE OF THE RIVER THAMES
A433
Thames Head
Kemble Station
Kemble
FROM ABOVE

centre.

The Path runs with the water up to a stile at the side of Upper Mill Farm. Keep sharp left to cross the mill race and turn right upstream. Beyond a stile leading to a field there is a view of Kemble's church spire. The Path now stays beside the river as far as Ewen. On the way there are a couple of stiles, a winding stretch (ignore the gate ahead) and a young wood flanked by stiles. The path crosses a stile in front of the attractive Brookside before reaching a stile at the road. Go right over the bridge leaving the river to flow alone. The lane passes the front of Brookside at the bend before reaching a T-junction in Ewen. The pub is to the right.

EWEN means 'source of a river'. The Source is still some distance away but Mill Farm at the west end had the last (or first) mill on the river - the water table has only fallen in modern times with gravel and water extraction. The village had a chapel until it was taken down to provide the south chapel of the restored Kemble Church in 1877. Ewen Manor is Georgian.

The Thames Path continues to the left along the road. Just past Mill Farm, and by the village sign, continue behind the hedge on the left to find the Thames joining to the left. When the path returns to the road go left for a few yards to Parker's Bridge. Do not cross the river but turn right down a step to follow the river. Round a bend, beyond a barn, there is a gate set back from the river to pass through. Stay by the river (with some young trees to the right) to reach the Kemble-Cirencester road on the edge of Kemble (left).

KEMBLE is a quiet village with an outstanding Brunel railway station built when this was a junction with a line to Cirencester. The local landmark is the church's stone spire resting on a 13th-century tower.

At the road cross over and bear right to find that the river has crossed at an angle. Go over the stile by the bridge. After a short distance cross a footbridge over a (usually dry) tributary. (To reach Kemble Station do not cross the footbridge but follow the path up to a road and turn left.)

The Thames Path follows the river bank for about 200 yards to a lonely tree. Here bear half left away from the water to walk close to the hedge over to the left. Go through the gate. (Over to the right is a low stone wall with openings at its base for the Thames, often boosted by the nearby spring, to flow through.) Continue ahead on high ground by the hedge. On coming level with a solitary house (over to the right) curve round to the right to join the shallow indentation of the tiny Thames which is usually dry by now. However, here at Thames Head, the Thames sometimes forms a lake in winter just below the Foss Way embankment. As the field opens out go forward to find steps leading up to the road. On the right is the tunnel for the infant Thames.

THAMES HEAD The high up main road is the Roman built Cirencester-Bath Foss Way. Thames Head Bridge, 200 yards east, carries the road over the former Thames & Severn Canal next to Thames Head Wharf where barges from London were unloaded.

Cross the main Cirencester road to a gap almost opposite and go up to a gate set back from the road. Climb over the stile on the right to reach the far side of the gate and follow the side of the field (left). The Thames valley is to the right. At the far end of the field go through the squeeze stile by a gate. The stone wall to the right of the gate is built to allow water to flow underneath when the Thames is in flood. Ahead can be seen the tower of Coates church. Follow the line of trees (right) up the valley to a stile by a gate. Bear half right to find, under an ash tree, a stone marking the source of the Thames.

THE SOURCE is marked by a simple stone placed here in 1974 by the Conservators of the River Thames who that year became part of the Thames Water Authority. Old Father Thames, now at St John's Lock, stood here from 1958 to 1974. Although the source usually appears dry there is of course water not far below the surface. The steep bank behind is the former Thames & Severn Canal.

To Reach Kemble Station

Retrace the way back to just before the second road and go right. Follow a slightly raised path by the old railway embankment (left) to a stile and continue to a second stile at a road. Turn left to go uphill and right into the station approach.

To Follow The Old Canal To Pub

Continue past the Thames source stone (right). A stone wall curves away over to the left near the isolated Tarltonfield Barn on high ground. Go over the stile ahead by the gate and follow the field boundary (right). At the next two gates there are ladderstiles. When the path rises to go over the canal do not cross the bridge but go left to go down on to the towpath of the former Thames & Severn Canal. Soon after passing under the Kemble-Gloucester railway line there is a former gate stop and round house built for canal staff. Beyond another bridge there is a deep cut leading to the Sapperton Tunnel entrance. Above is The Tunnel House Inn.

TUNNEL HOUSE INN was built in local stone at the instigation of the Earl of Bathurst for workmen digging the tunnel in the 1780s. Many were miners from Derbyshire and Cornwall. The canal tunnel is over 2 miles long and took 5 years to build with men working day and night by candlelight. When completed it took 4 or 5 hours for the leggers, who lay on their backs and used their legs on the walls, to take a barge through. The men often suffered from a complaint known as 'lighterman's bottom'. The last boat passed through in 1911. One of the niches at this southern portal of the tunnel was intended for the figure of Old Father Thames. The pub has survived and in the Fifties was visited by the poet John Betjeman. Today it is full of interesting historic clutter with the main bar like a drawing room complete with log fire in winter. There are mud scrapers at the door for walkers to use before entering.

Refreshments

Cricklade: Cricklade Café & Restaurant, High Street (01793 750368). Open Mon-Sat 8am-8pm (9.30pm Fri & Sat); Sun 10am-3pm.

Ashton Keynes: The Plough Inn, Back Street (on Thames Path). 7-10.30pm daily; also 12-3pm weekends.

Ewen: The Wild Duck. Built in 1563. Real Ales. 11am-11pm. (Sun 12-10.30pm.)

Coates (canal beyond Source): The Tunnel House. Real Ales, meals and snacks. Children welcome. 11am-3pm & 6-11pm. All day Sat. (Sun 12-10.30pm.)

Accommodation

Cricklade: The White Lion, High Street (01793 750443).

Cricklade: 23 High Street (01793 750205). Dinner available.

Waterhay Bridge: Waterhay Farm, Leigh, SN6 6QY (01285 861253). Cross bridge and turn right.

Ashton Keynes: Corner Cottage, Fore Street, SN6 6NP (01285 861454).

Ashton Keynes: 2 Cove House, east of The White Hart (01285 861221). Dinner available.

Ashton Keynes: The Plough Inn, Back Street (on Thames Path). Camping allowed in summer.

Ewen: The Wild Duck Inn (01285 770310). Built in 1563.

Kemble: Smerrill Barns, GL7 6BW (01285 770907). Right along main Kemble-Cirencester road for $^1/_2$ mile and not left into village.

Coates (canal beyond Source): The Tunnel House. Camping facilities (01285 770280).

Transport

Cricklade: Rail (Great Western/Thames Trains) to Swindon then bus (Stagecoach 51).

Source: Rail from Kemble (Wales & West/Great Western).

Map

OS Landranger 163 (Cheltenham).

BIBLIOGRAPHY

Banks, Leslie and Stanley, Christopher: *The Thames: A history from the Air* (Oxford 1990).

Belloc, Hilaire: *The Historic Thames 1907* (Webb & Bower 1988).

Chaplin, Peter H: *The Thames from Source to Tideway* (Whittet Books 1982).

Dickens, Charles (jun): *Dictionary of the Thames* (Dickens & Evans 1893).

Ebel, Suzanne and Impey, Doreen: *A Guide to London's Riverside* (Constable 1985).

Elsom, Derek: *Taming the Rivers of Oxford* (Oxford Region Thematic Trails, Oxford Polytechnic 1987).

Hatts, Leigh: *Country Walks Around London* (David & Charles 1983).

Hatts, Leigh: *Pub Walks Along The Thames Path* (Countryside Books 1997).

Hatts, Leigh: *The Thames Walk: Feasibility Report* (Countryside Commission 1984).

Hatts, Leigh: *Walks Along The Thames Path* (PSL/Haynes 1990).

Hayward, Graham: *Stanford's River Thames Companion* (Stanford 1988).

Hibbert, Christopher and Hibbert, Edward: *The Encyclopaedia of Oxford* (Macmillan 1988).

Jebb, Miles: *A Guide to the Thames Path* (Constable 1988).

Jenkins, Alan: *The Book of The Thames* (Papermac 1983).

Jerome, Jerome K: *Three Men in a Boat* annotated by Christopher Matthew & Benny Green (Pavilion 1982).

Leapman, Michael: *London's River: A History of the Thames* (Pavilion 1991).

Leyland, John: *The Thames Illustrated* (Newnes 1901).

Livingston, Helen: *The Thames Path: Aerofilms Guide* (Ian Allan 1993).

Mackay, Duncan: *The Secret Thames* (Ebury 1992).

Pevsner, Nikolaus: *The Buildings Of England county series* (Penguin).

Phillips, Geoffrey: *Thames Crossings* (David & Charles 1981).

Pritchard, Mari and Carpenter, Humphrey: *A Thames Companion* (Oxford 1975).

Rodgers, David: *William Morris At Home* (Ebury 1996).

Sharp, David: *The Thames Walk* (Ramblers' Association 1990).

Taunt, Henry: *New Map of the Thames 1872* (Alan Sutton 1989).

Weinreb, Ben and Hibbert, Christopher: *The London Encyclopaedia* (Macmillan 1983).

Wilson, D.G.: *The Thames: Record of a Working Waterway* (Batsford 1987).

The Royal River: The Thames from Source to Sea 1885 (Bloomsbury Books 1985).

Dockland: Historical Survey (NELP/GLC 1986).

The Thames Path: Proposed Long Distance Path (Countryside Commission 1989).